THE
STUDY
OF
RELIGION
AND
PRIMITIVE
RELIGIONS

RELIGION AND MAN

Under the General Editorship of
W. RICHARD COMSTOCK

THE STUDY OF RELIGION AND PRIMITIVE RELIGIONS

W. RICHARD COMSTOCK
University of California at Santa Barbara

Harper & Row, Publishers
New York, Evanston, San Francisco, London

Cover photo: Allen Hagood, National Park Service

RELIGION AND MAN:
THE STUDY OF RELIGION AND PRIMITIVE RELIGIONS

Copyright © 1972 by Harper & Row, Publishers, Inc.

Standard Book Number: 06-041338-7

Library of Congress Catalog Card Number: 76-185899

CONTENTS

PREFACE

Religion is a persistent and pervasive feature of the continuing history of mankind. To some it is a superstitious barrier to man's progress; to others it is his most constructive activity providing an ultimate meaning to the projects of his culture. What is beyond controversy is the importance of appreciating the force of religion as a major influence in the life of man.

The present volume provides an introduction to the scholarly study of some of the religious traditions involved in human history. It can be read alone or as part of a three-volume paperback series which is also available in a one-volume hardbound edition. The authors of these volumes have sought to provide accurate descriptions of the rituals, myths, symbolic devices, belief systems, and social organizations of the world's religions. They have also provided sensitive interpretations of the ethos and the spiritual directions to which these various symbolic forms have pointed. In doing so the authors show how a religious tradition can be studied in such a way that both data and interpretation, fact and meaning, detail and the patterns unifying the detail into a dynamic whole can be recognized and appreciated.

Alfred North Whitehead once wrote: "The death of religion comes with the repression of the high hope of adventure." This volume is an impressive illustration of the fact that in the field of the study of the religious traditions of mankind this spirit of adventure is far from dead.

W. Richard Comstock

THE
STUDY
OF
RELIGION
AND
PRIMITIVE
RELIGIONS

APPROACHES TO THE STUDY OF RELIGION

Religion reveals a fascinating panorama of variegated forms. A tribal man lifts his hands in ecstatic celebration of the sun as the giver of warmth and light; another seeks a spell whereby his wife may be cured of an illness caused by a witch. In India, a holy man sits as he has sat for many years in unmoving contemplation of the Nameless Reality that is his own self; another seeks to use the power of "soul force" to change traditional social patterns that have caused unnecessary misery to his people. In China, a nobleman meditates on the "way" of the universe and seeks to conform to its rhythms in his own being. In Japan, after many years of preparation, an aspirant experiences the moment of Zen enlightenment. In the West, a rabbi meditates on the "law" of God; a congregation gathers on Easter morning to reaffirm the resurrection of its Lord; pilgrims fulfill a vow by making their way to Mecca.

Celebration, despair, ethical vigor, mystic retreat, social activism, monastic quietude, contemplation, animal sacrifice, rituals involving pain and terror, images of hope, symbols of fear, the affirmation of life and the struggle against death, creative growth, unthinking superstition—all these are included in the phenomenon that we call religion. Can such a protean phenomenon be studied according to careful methods that will provide reliable knowledge? At first glance, imposing obstacles seem to stand in the way of such a project.

First, the prospective student may be overwhelmed by the sheer enormity of the subject. The study of religion encompasses a geographical spread that includes Eurasia, Africa, Australia, the South Sea Islands, and the Americas, as well as a temporal spread that begins in the dim paleolithic past and reaches down to the present state of creative flux. Finally, there is a qualitative diversity among the kinds of phenomena that we tend to call religion within a single geographical area at a given segment of time. Religion can refer to subjective experiences like feelings of sacred awe or mystical visions; social facts like the existence of Christian churches and Buddhist congregations called the *sangha;* symbolic systems (communication systems of signs) that include forms like the cross and the swastika as well as beliefs expressed in various theologies and philosophies of religion; ritual acts like a sacred dance or the performance of an ablutionary rite; ethical norms and prescriptions for desired behavior; ideals for a more humane life in this world; techniques for obtaining happiness in another world. The list of religious forms seems almost endless.

Further perplexities are generated by the way that public acts and practices are intertwined with the private emotions, subjective meanings, and personal interpretations of those participating in the acts. Religion seems to mean so many different things to people in different parts of the world. How can we ever hope to capture these meanings in conceptual formulas that will be understandable and acceptable to all concerned?

In the past few centuries scholars from a number of fields—psychology, sociology, anthropology, and history—have studied the phenomena of religion in ways that have led to impressive results. They have produced a body of empirical descriptions of the religions of the world that have increased our knowledge of what the members of the world's religions think and do. Furthermore, these scholars have worked out a number of methods for the study of religion that offer ways of overcoming the difficulties we have noted. In Part 1 of this book we propose to consider ways of studying religion that have been found to be especially rewarding.

The first task in the study of religion is to learn how to ask the right questions. We can only obtain good answers to questions that have been properly formed, because the form of the question determines the kind of answer given. The well-known question "When did you stop beating your wife?" is difficult for some men to answer because the question already prescribes the range of possible answers and prevents the party in question from denying that he has ever beaten his wife at all. In the study of religion one needs to learn how to ask questions that lead to fruitful results and to avoid questions that are unproductive.

The American philosopher George Santayana once observed that those who do not know history are doomed to repeat its errors. This point has its application in the area that we are considering. Scholars who have studied religion in the nineteenth and twentieth centuries have asked a number of questions about religion and have found some of them to be more fruitful than others. Many of these questions will also occur to a student beginning his study of this complex subject. In this connection a preliminary survey of the work that has already been accomplished in this field can be extremely useful. If we see what questions have already been considered and why some of them have proved to be more useful than others, it may save a lot of time and start us on a fruitful course of study.

In the nineteenth and early twentieth centuries great progress was made in the development of sociology and anthropology. Many of the pioneers in these fields devoted a great deal of attention to religion, because they found that religion played a significant role in the various societies that they studied. Without knowledge of the place of religion in human society, any account of how a society was formed and operated proved to be incomplete. During this period the field of psychology also made great strides and a similar situation regarding religion was encountered. Whatever the personal attitudes of the investigator toward religion might be, he found that religious ideas and motives operated in the psychology of the people he studied and had to be included in any full account of the springs of their behavior.

THE QUESTION OF RELIGIOUS ORIGINS

The pioneers in these fields provided accounts of religion that are still useful, though they must be qualified in the light of more recent and exact information. If we summarize in a very general way one common feature of these approaches, we can recognize that they tended to be interested in the question of the "origin" of religion. Although they differed among themselves as to the exact answer, they agreed at the methodological level that this was a proper and rewarding question to ask.

In the nineteenth century many anthropologists, classical scholars, and philologists advocated an approach to religion that was called the nature-myth school. According to this school the great symbols of the world's religions were personifications of natural phenomena: the sun, moon, stars, storms, the seasons of the year. Advocates of this approach argued among themselves about which force of nature was primary in the concerns of early religion. One branch maintained that solar myths were most important and that primitive rituals and myths were primarily concerned with man's relation to the sun. Max Müller (1823–1900), a philologist who did pioneer work in the study of Indo-European languages, advocated this approach. He developed the method of "comparative religion" and tried to show how nature myths operated in both European religions and the religions of India.

One of the great pioneers in the field of anthropology is Edward Tylor (1832–1917). Tylor argued that religion had its origin in the belief in immaterial souls that might inhabit objects like stones, trees, animals, or human bodies, but which also could exist independently of them. He coined the word *animism* (after the Greek word *anima,* "soul") to refer to the belief in the existence of such transempirical souls or spirits. Tylor further argued that the origin of this belief was probably in dreams. For example, a man may dream of a friend who has recently died. In the dream the man seems to continue to exist as a soul independent of his physical body. Through dream experiences, man thus became convinced of the ex-

A shaman's painted leather leggings, probably from the Tshimshian tribe. (Courtesy of the American Museum of Natural History.)

istence of a realm of spirit entities which are the basis of religious beliefs.

The philosopher Herbert Spencer (1820–1903) offered a similar theory with some variations. Spencer found the origin of religion in the respect given to ancestors combined with the belief in ghosts caused by dream experiences. Spencer held that man makes the ghosts of his ancestors into gods. Thus "ancestor-worship is the root of every religion." This theory is sometimes called euhemerism after a fourth century B.C. thinker named Euhemerus who argued that the gods of religion were originally living men of great power and authority who were raised to the status of divine beings.

James Frazer (1854–1941) was a classical scholar who collected a great deal of material on religion and wrote a very influential study in many volumes called *The Golden Bough*. Frazer argued that religion developed out of an original magical stage of human culture. Frazer saw the primitive magician as a person who wants to know how the universe operates and how it can be controlled for human purposes. According to Frazer, the magician mistakes superficial relations between objects for the real underlying causal relations between them discovered by the modern scientist. Nevertheless, the magician is like the modern scientist in his desire to understand how phenomena can be understood and controlled. The magician is simply a primitive scientist who has made mistakes due to insufficient knowledge and techniques. Frazer held that magic and religion are distinct phenomena though related through a process of historical development. The magician believes that phenomena can be controlled through magic spells. The religious man believes in the existence of spirits that must be placated and cajoled by prayers, rather than controlled directly through a magic formula. Nevertheless, the religionist is like the magician in that both seek to explain how the natural world works.

The theories advanced by Tylor, Spencer, and Frazer assume that religion is primarily an attempt to answer questions about the world that are similar in kind to those asked by a modern scientist. The primitive religionist has made a hypothesis on the basis of insufficient evidence. Nevertheless, his beliefs are products of thought though they have reached erroneous conclusions. According to this view, religion has its origin in an intellectual mistake.

These theories stressing an intellectual origin were soon opposed by another group of theories that stressed the emotional aspects of religion. Tylor and Frazer were not unaware of this feature, but other anthropologists insisted more emphatically that it was in the emotions that the origins of religion are to be found. Thus R. R. Marett (1866–1943) argued that religion is not so much an intellectual endeavor as a set of profound emotional responses to various aspects of human existence.

Wilhelm Wundt (1832–1920), a psychologist, argued that in religion emotions like fear "are projected outward into the environment." A philosopher, Rudolf Otto (1869–1937), wrote an influential book called the *Idea of the Holy*. Otto did not mean "idea" in an intellectualist sense. He was rather referring to a form of perception (in the sense meant by Immanuel Kant) which he called the "numinous" and which was characterized by affective tones of the awesome, the mysterious, and the fascinating. Otto did not call the numinous an emotion, but other investigators have adapted his analysis to the thesis that a distinctive emotion conveying a sense of the mysterious, the uncanny, and the sacred is the basis of religion. Others, like William James (1842–1910), have denied that there is a distinctive religious emotion as such, but they have believed that religion has its origins in profound emotional experiences related to beliefs in spirits, gods, and a supernatural world.

These early theories about the origins of religion assumed two forms. At one level, the question of origins dealt with certain structural constants in human psychology that were alleged to be the cause of the rise of religion in human life and culture. The intellectual theories argued that man's mind is such that he inevitably tries out magical or religious hypotheses about the nature of the world and then turns to science when greater knowledge and more sophisticated methods of investigation are finally at his disposal. In similar fashion, emotional theories aver that human psychology is such that certain emotional responses and needs lead to religious practices as expressions of those emotions.

However, at another level, the question about origins is a historical one that looks for the form of religion as it actually appeared in the human past. In the eighteenth century Charles de Brosses

(1709–1777) argued that the first form of religion was fetishism (the worship of inanimate objects like stones, and animate objects like trees and animals). Tylor believed that the first form was animism, or the belief in "souls" distinct from the material objects that the souls might inhabit. Frazer believed that a magic stage preceded the animistic one.

R. R. Marett did a great deal to popularize the view that the stage of animism was preceded by a stage in which primitive man believed in the existence of a general power or force that pervaded both inanimate and animate objects. He was influenced in this point by the work of Robert Henry Codrington (1830–1922), a missionary who had pointed out how the Melanesians referred to "mana" as a kind of power which could produce extraordinary occurrences in nature and also enable man to perform acts beyond his normal capacity. Other primitive tribes have similar conceptions. Among the American Indians, the Sioux refer to "wakenda," the Iroquois to "orenda," and the Algonquin to "manitu" in ways similar to the Melanesian "mana." Marett argued that the belief in mana probably preceded the belief in specific souls that operated at the animistic stage.

A popular evolutionary scheme imposed on these foundations held that religion then developed from the stage of animism (perhaps preceded by a stage of fetishism, magic, or belief in mana) to polytheism, or the belief in souls that have assumed the shape and power of independent gods; this in turn was followed by a henotheistic stage in which one god is held to be more powerful than the others, and finally a monotheistic stage emerges in which one god only is believed to exist and possess absolute power.

On the other hand, Wilhelm Schmidt (1868–1954) and Andrew Lang (1844–1912) argued independently that this scheme distorted the actual facts because it can be shown that belief in a high god or supreme being (the characteristic of monotheism) is by no means a late development. They argued that primitive societies possessing the most simple and rudimentary technology disclose the belief in high gods and often in a supreme God who is the creator of the world. Schmidt thus argued for a scheme of development beginning with a primordial monotheism that later changed (i.e., either developed or degenerated, according to one's point of view) into polytheism, animism, and magic.

Schmidt's view did not gain wide acceptance at the time, but a later generation of investigators has accepted the validity of a great deal of his data about the existence of the belief in high gods in very primitive cultures. Thus Schmidt has shown that an evolutionary scheme based on the supposed existence of some original stage of pure animism, magic, and polytheism is not supported by our present knowledge. No such stage has been found. But neither has a stage of original monotheism been uncovered. All of these evolutionary schemes have remained as speculative hypotheses that can neither be proved or disproved. In any known culture, whether primitive or modern, we find all or most of these elements existing side by side. No method has yet been worked out whereby we can decide on the temporal priority of some of them to others.

We have seen how one group of early theories about religion can be divided between the intellectual and emotional approaches. Another group of theories about the origin of religion can be similarly divided into sociological and psychological approaches.

SOCIOLOGICAL AND PSYCHOLOGICAL THEORIES

Emile Durkheim (1858–1917), one of the pioneers in the development of sociology as a scientific discipline, is a representative of the former. In a still useful book entitled *The Elementary Forms of the Religious Life,* Durkheim argued that religious systems of thought and behavior are so pervasive in human culture that it is difficult to believe that they are simply the result of an intellectual mistake or that they deal with purely imaginary concerns. Durkheim believed that, on the contrary, the religions of man deal with a very real empirical object. That object is human society which exists on the concrete plane of human experience as the web of human relations, imposing on each individual man rules of conduct that determine the shape of his social life. Society thus confronts the individual as a force that requires man to behave in ways that often go against his personal inclinations. Nevertheless, since man is a social creature, he finds that he must integrate his personal life into the larger life of the community as a whole. Durkheim argued that religion is one of the ways in which man accomplishes this socialization process. The symbols of religion appear to their users to be about a realm of supernatural powers and forces. They are really about society and its claims on the individual. The laws of a god are really the most crucial laws of a given society.

Durkheim then tied this social theory of religion to a particular theory about the historical origins of religion. Durkheim was intrigued by the phenomenon of totemism, i.e., the practice of taking a particular natural object or animal and making it into the symbol (or totem) of a particular social group called a clan. Durkheim believed that in totemism the social nature of religion as well as its social origin was clearly demonstrated. The totem figures clearly represented social groups and at the same time led to the belief in distinctive gods and spirits ruling over men.

On the other hand, Sigmund Freud (1856–1939) is an influential representative of theories of religion that emphasize psychological factors. Freud argued that the origin of religion can be found in the problems of the child seeking to work out adequate relationships with his parents, particularly his father. At first the child considers his father to be a figure of absolute power. When he learns that his father is human—all too human—with definite limitations to both his benevolence and his power, the youth feels deprived of the psychological support and security he felt as a small child. He therefore projects onto the universe a belief in a cosmic father or god who can continue to give him the support he once had from his human father.

Freud also gave this theory a historical form. He suggested that primitive man originally existed in patriarchal societies where the father-leader kept all desirable females to himself. At some point the sons rebelled, killed the father, and took his women as their own wives. However, this primal act and its ensuing guilt are the psychological cause of belief in a father-god whose wrath has to be placated through sacrifice.

Another equally speculative theory opposing this one was advanced by writers like Johann Bachofen (1815–1887). Bachofen argued that matriarchal societies preceded patriarchal ones and that the first form of religion was worship of mother figures. Father-gods then supplanted the goddesses of primordial antiquity as men wrested the control of society from its matriarchal leaders. Although such a theory is of special interest to literary people, anthropologists have not been able to establish the existence of a primal stage in which only female divinities were worshiped.

It is not necessary here to provide a detailed analysis of the strengths and weaknesses of these various theories. The point for the beginning student of religion to recognize is that all of them remain at the level of speculative hypotheses which have neither been proved nor disproved, since there is no method presently available whereby we can uncover and demonstrate the existence of a stage in human culture where only fetishism, animism, belief in mana, totemism, or a belief in high gods exists. The occurrence of some primal act like Freud's belief in the murder of the father-patriarch has never been demonstrated as a historical fact. What can be studied as social facts are primitive and modern cultures in which religious forms already operate with all or some of these factors in dynamic interaction. It is impossible to say which of them is primary or the origin of the others.

By the same token, no method has yet been devised whereby we can isolate the one factor in the human make-up that can clearly be designated as the single source of man's religious activity. In any existing religious form we can detect elements of thought and feeling, belief and emotion, psychological and social factors, that are inextricably connected. The quest for origins forces us to simplify and distort these very complex phenomena. Each of these theories contains some true insights into how a particular religious form operates. No one of them alone seems to give the basic principle on which all the other aspects of religious activity are based.

For these reasons, the next generation of scholars producing important work in the twentieth century has largely abandoned the quest for the origins of religion. It is not that the questions raised are not interesting or important. On the contrary, much of the material considered by the scholars we have just surveyed remains useful. However, the method of approach has changed. The quest for origins has been superseded by a quest for more adequate description. A different question is now being asked. Instead of asking, "What is the origin of religion?" scholars now tend to ask: "How does religion function?" "What is it like?" "What does it do for the individual or for his society?"

In other words, a more empirical approach to religion is now being adopted. The question as to how religion originated is a speculative question, difficult to answer in a scientific way. But the fact remains that religion does exist as a very concrete factor in human experience and behavior. May it not be more fruitful to accept it as a "given" which it is our task to examine according to the best analytical tools and methods of accurate description that can be devised?

In the twentieth century investigators of religion in a variety of disciplines have turned in the main from the question of the origins of religion to the question of the description of religion. Instead of asking what the ultimate cause of religion is, they now ask what religion as it presently exists is like.

THE QUESTION OF THE DESCRIPTION OF RELIGION

This new question involves the investigator in certain problems of method. What is it that he is studying? We may answer, religious phenomena or facts. But then we must decide what is the proper method for studying a religious fact. Contemporary scholars tend to approach this problem in two related ways. First of all, in studying religion we are studying things that men *do*. In their society and in their personal life they behave in certain ways and make certain things that we characterize as religious. The study of religion has therefore a concrete observable content: specific kinds of human behavior called religious. It is this situation that makes religion susceptible to careful study according to the methods of scholars and scientists. Religion may or may not be about something superempirical that transcends human life. Religion is not itself that superempirical reality. It is a human phenomenon—something that men do —which can be observed and carefully described.

Second, since these acts are human acts, they involve a characteristic that is not present in the realm of inanimate physical objects. This characteristic is the element of symbolism and meaning. Human actions mean something, both to the person performing the action and to those responding to his action. Therefore, in the description of any human action, it is never sufficient to describe the surface details of the action as they appear to sense observation. We must also include a description of what the action means to the one performing it.

For example, suppose that we observe a man stretching his hands out in front of his face. It is not enough to record the physical movements involved. A full account must include the meaning of that act. Perhaps the man is shielding his face from the sun. Perhaps he is warding off some external object, like a shrub or an insect. Perhaps he is invoking a god in a religious rite. Perhaps he is greeting a friend, according to the custom of his particular society. Such considerations of meaning must be included in any complete description of the act in question.

Contemporary scholars of religion have become increasingly aware of these factors. Therefore the question of adequate religious descriptions has taken two dominant forms. One, many psychologists and sociologists ask functional questions. In a given religious act, what is man doing? What does the religious symbol or rite do for him or for his society? What kinds of problems does it solve for him?

Two, many students of human language and culture ask hermeneutical questions. What does a given religious symbol mean? How is a practice to be interpreted? What is its significance in the society where it is used?

Functional and hermeneutical approaches are not mutually exclusive. On the contrary, most scholars at the present time ask questions about religion in which both are involved. Indeed, in the final analysis, they are really two aspects of the same approach. Furthermore, the observation of a fact requires an observer. An observer, in turn, must look at his material from a particular point of observation, which we can call a vantage point or perspective. What we are able to see in any given case depends on the perspective from which we choose to observe it. Functional and hermeneutical approaches must thus face this problem of perspectives.

This leads us to the perplexing problem of cultural perspectives. The observer of a given religious phenomenon is often looking at it from outside of the specific cultural perspective adopted by those performing the particular rite or adopting the particular symbol in question. Some scholars have consequently wondered if the observer can describe the phenomenon in a way that truly captures what it means to the participants. This is a serious problem presently being discussed by philosophers. However, one point should be stressed. The difficulty should not be associated with the perplexing problem of how an observer can appreciate the inner subjective experiences of another person. The student of religion is not studying the subjectivity of other people directly. Rather he is studying their objective acts and symbols which are observable. His task is one of hermeneutics, i.e., how to interpret the meanings that are meant to be conveyed by these acts and symbols. This task is difficult, but not nearly so difficult as somehow getting "inside" the mind of the other. The latter is not necessary. All that is required is that the student make a fair interpretation of the other's meaning as indicated in his overt expressions and acts. This is possible because man's symbolic acts can be interpreted when put into a proper context, just as we can understand what is meant by a handshake if we know something of the cultural context of rules and customs in which it occurs.

Perhaps a story will illustrate the kind of situation meant and the problems that it poses. Two men were having a religious discussion. One man asked: "Do you believe in infant baptism?" The other replied: "Believe in it? I've actually seen it!" The humor in this story depends on a deliberate confusion of perspectives. The second man had adopted the perspective of physical observation. What has he seen? A man applying water to an infant in the presence of some other persons. But the first man asked his question from a different perspective. He assumes knowledge of the physical act, but wants to know if his friend also viewed the fact from a perspective of certain religious meanings, i.e., that this act had included the child in a specific community (the church), that the members of the church believe it to be part of a divine plan ordained by God. The observer does not himself have to believe in the claims made from that perspective. Nevertheless, to describe what has happened, he must be aware of the perspective and include it in his account of the meaning.

So far we have considered in a general way the contemporary approach to religion through a concern with the description of religious acts and meanings. However, such categories—religious acts and meanings—are still too broad in their scope. The student of religion must learn how to adopt a narrower methodological perspective from which specific questions about religion can be asked and answered. At the present time we can distinguish in the voluminous studies of religion by contemporary scholars at least five basic methodological perspectives.

METHODOLOGICAL PERSPECTIVES

First is the *psychological* perspective. Each individual man has personal problems involving the way that he handles his various "drives"—his need for sexual satisfaction, friendship, acceptance by his peers, prestige and power, a sense that his life has importance and value. Psychologists have examined how religious symbols and practices aid or impede the individual in working out these problems.

Within the field of contemporary psychology a number of different schools exist and the approach to religion is partly determined by the psychological presuppositions that are held. Freud interpreted religion primarily as a neurotic solution to feelings of infantile dependency. However, even those disagreeing with Freud on this point find in his work a mine of valuable materials about how religion operates in human attempts to solve problems in the relation of a man to his father, mother, and other authority figures.

Carl Jung (1875–1961) disagreed with Freud's estimation of religion and argued that man had a need to find "meaning" in his life which often assumed a religious form. He also investigated archetypal symbols that appeared in human dreams and which were similar to symbols appearing in the world's religions. Jung believed that these symbols often aided the individual in working out problems concerning the integration of his personality. Other psychologists, from other points of view, have also stressed the role religion plays in finding a meaning for life. Erik Erikson (1902–   ) has done impressive work in showing how the quest for personal identity is often worked out in a religious way.

A second perspective is the *sociological* one. Sociologists have made the basic unit of their study not the individual personality but the network of relations among people binding them together in cohesive groups called societies. They have studied how religion operates at the social level to solve a number of related problems. First, a given religion may itself possess a social structure that must be maintained from generation to generation. Then, too, the religion may operate in the larger structure of some social unit like the tribe or nation and help or impede that society in maintaining its social existence. Finally, a given religion may help or impede the individual in integrating his personal life into the larger life of the society of which he is a part.

Social anthropologists have made important contributions to the study of how religion operates in human society, particularly in primitive (or preliterate) societies. These anthropologists illustrate in an exceptionally striking manner the transition from the quest for religious origins to the quest for religious descriptions that we have noted. The scholars who worked out early theories of origins—men like Tylor and Frazer—depended on reports from missionaries, travelers, and colonial administrators. They did not themselves observe the cultures that they described. Anthropology developed as a scientific discipline by stressing the need for field work and firsthand observations of the cultures being studied. One pioneer in developing adequate techniques of observation and description was Bronislaw Malinowski (1884–1942), whose studies of religious activities (among many other dimensions of human culture) in the Trobriander Islands are still very valuable. A. R. Radcliffe-Brown (1881–1955) has made important contributions to methodological theory. He developed a structural approach (which should be distinguished from the "structuralism" of Claude Lévi-Strauss, considered in a later chapter). Radcliffe-Brown argued that a society should not be considered as a mere aggregate or collection of people who happen to be together. Rather a society exhibits a social structure delineating the way the behavior of people is "connected by a definite set of social relations into an integrated whole." [1] The study of a given society is the study of the totality of its interacting parts, of how family relations, legal forms, political structures, religious practices, artistic expressions, mores, and customs contribute to the successful functioning of social life as a whole. Thus:

The function of culture as a whole is to unite individual human beings into more or less stable social structures, i.e., stable systems of groups determining and regulating the relation of those individuals to one another, and providing such external adaptation to the physical environment, and such internal adaptation between the component individuals or groups, as to make possible an ordered social life. [2]

This general structural approach leads to a functional method in the study of religion as with all other social forms as well. A functional method does not ask what religion is or what its origins are. It rather asks, what is the function of religion in the social complex of which it is a part? How does religion contribute to social integration? According to this method, one can also ask questions about

1. Quoted in E. E. Evans-Pritchard, *Social Anthropology,* New York, Cohen & West, 1954, p. 54. See bibliography for works on structuralism in sociology.
2. Quoted in ibid., p. 55.

negative function (or dysfunction), i.e., how does religion at times contribute to social disintegration and conflict?

Radcliffe-Brown's theory is one influential approach among many that have been developed by anthropologists and sociologists. Pioneers in the development of sociology like Emile Durkheim and Max Weber (1864–1920) have produced valuable studies of the way religion operates in society. Talcott Parsons (1902–   ) has developed a general scheme of a human action system. According to this scheme, man performs his acts within four subsystems. First is the cultural system of meanings, intentions, norms, and patterns of human behavior; second is the social system, which deals with the patterns of interaction and order among social groups; third is the personality system, which deals with the individual goals of the members of a society; fourth is the organic system directed to the biological needs. Parsons then distinguishes in addition two "environments" in which human action takes place. One is the realm of physical nature; the other is the realm of "ultimate reality." Here Parsons is not making the claim that such a realm necessarily exists; he is rather pointing out that man in society does, in fact, usually fashion his patterns of concrete behavior in such a way that they are validated through reference to ultimate principles that often take a religious form.

According to Parsons, "the cultural system structures commitments vis-à-vis ultimate reality into meaningful orientations toward the rest of the environment and the organismic system similarly adapts itself and the other systems to the physical environment." [3] Religions can then be studied according to the way they operate (or function) in this system of human action.

A third methodological approach to religion is a *historical* one. Psychological and sociological approaches tend to be ahistorical in the sense that they are primarily interested in examining how a religion functions at a given period of time for the human individual or in the society of which he is a part. However, man also exists in a human world that has gone through a series of transformations in time. Historians therefore study the behavior of man through the sequence of events by which various forms of life have come into being and others have passed away. While the historian does not look for ultimate origins, he is interested not only in what presently exists, but in the historical process by which existing forms have assumed their present shape.

It is useful then to consider a given religion as a specific tradition of beliefs and practices that has gone through a complex course of development and transformation. We can apply the methods of historiography to that religion and provide as accurate and thorough an account as is possible of what this historical development has been like.

So far as religion is concerned, this requires the efforts of historians trained in the collection and interpretation of documents that

3. Talcott Parsons, *Societies*, Englewood Cliffs, N.J., Prentice-Hall, 1966, p. 9.

reveal the past history of civilizations. It also involves the work of scholars primarily concerned with languages, classicists and orientalists who can read the documents and artifacts of ancient cultures with facility and understanding. Linguists and philologists make important contributions as do archeologists who interpret cultural artifacts as well as written documents.

It is obvious that the history of religions encompasses a very wide field. Many historians of religion are specialists in a single area, like the history of Indian religions or the religions of Greece and Rome. Others, like Raffaele Pettazzoni (1883–1960), seek to develop a comprehensive knowledge of the entire field. The "History of Religions" school at Chicago, represented by Mircea Eliade (1907–   ) and others, seeks to be faithful to religious phenomena in their full complexity.

The fourth methodological approach to religion is a *form-comparative* one. By a religious form we mean a specific religious phenomenon that reveals a distinctive structure of its own and which is capable of being compared or contrasted with others. This form might be a specific myth, like a certain story of how the world came into being; it might be a specific rite, like a form of animal sacrifice; it might be a specific religious functionary, like a shaman or a priest. The comparative approach first examines this form in one specific religious tradition and then compares it with what appear to be similar forms in other religious traditions. The difficulty in this perspective is how to decide when a similarity of form indicates an important relationship between the forms and when it is a superficial and essentially trivial resemblance. Scholars warn against a simplistic use of the comparative method that will obscure the concrete differences existing between the religion of one culture or historical tradition and another very different one.

Nevertheless, when applied cautiously, the method can be useful. Many scholars interested in comparative matters have been influenced by the philosophy of phenomenology developed by Edmund Husserl (1859–1938). Without accepting this philosophy as a whole, some students of religion have used its techniques to isolate specific "phenomena" of religion according to their essential forms. The "forms" are then studied in a comparative manner as they appear in various cultures. Important work using this approach has been done by Gerardus van der Leeuw (1890–1950) in his *Religion in Essence and Manifestation.* Although he was not a phenomenologist, Rudolf Otto's work is often cited as an example of the approach. For example, Otto's attempt to isolate a distinctive form of consciousness called the numinous is an example of how a specific "phenomenon" can be distinguished and then studied as it "appears" in a variety of cultures.

A fifth perspective is already involved in the other perspectives we have noted. However, it is so important that it merits a separate designation of its own. In a general way, we can characterize it as the hermeneutical or semiological approach. It includes a number of approaches to religion that disagree among themselves but which are united by a common interest in religions as systems of symbols, as kinds of languages that impart meanings which must be interpreted. Here scholars from a number of fields have made distinctive contributions.

For example, psychologists have been impressed by the way that man expresses his dilemmas through symbols. Thus Freud discovered that in his dreams the individual was actually expressing problems of personal and social adjustment through complex dream imagery. Jung developed the theory that dreams revealed archetypal forms (like the great mother or the venerable father) that also appeared in the great religions of the world.

Sociologists and anthropologists have similarly emphasized the importance of studying culture through its expression in symbols. Thus Max Weber approached societies as "systems of meaning" which must be interpreted through a method he called *verstehen*. E. E. Evans-Pritchard (1902–   ) declares that "social anthropology studies societies as moral, or symbolic, systems and not as natural systems . . . it is less interested in process than in design." [4]

Philosophers like Ernst Cassirer (1874–1945) and Susanne Langer (1895–   ) have studied human cultures as the media through which symbolic forms are expressed and which it is the task of the student to interpret. Cassirer was less interested in individual forms, like a specific myth, than in general symbolic structures, like a mythic form of thought, through which particular myths are presented.

In recent years the interest in symbolism has assumed a highly technical form. A French anthropologist, Claude Lévi-Strauss (1908–   ), has expounded the method of structuralism (to be distinguished from Radcliffe-Brown's use of the term). Lévi-Strauss's theory applies to human culture as a whole, but it has particular significance for the study of religion. Lévi-Strauss believes that religious myths and rituals are not the expression of blind emotions and undisciplined imagination. On the contrary, according to him they exhibit patterns and structures that possess logical order and precise relationships among the parts (this theory is dealt with in the discussion of symbolic expression in a later chapter).

These five methodological perspectives—the psychological, sociological, historical, comparative, and hermeneutical—provide useful ways to consider religion. In the following chapters we will consider a number of examples from the religions of tribal societies in which the combinations of these approaches, interacting with one another, help us to understand what is happening in typical religious acts.

4. Evans-Pritchard, op. cit., p. 62.

TOWARD
A DEFINITION
OF RELIGION

In discussing the nature of time, the Christian theologian Augustine once observed: "If you do not ask me what time is, I know; if you ask me I do not know." We may feel in a similar situation concerning the question, "What is religion?"

In the last chapter we considered how scholars have turned from the question of the origins of religion to the question of how it can be described. However, if the task of description does not require an answer to the problem of origins, does it not at least require a definition? Must we not define the kind of subject matter that we are attempting to study, before we can study it?

Max Weber answered this question in the negative. He declared: "To define 'religion,' to say what it *is* is not possible at the start of a presentation. . . . Definition can be attempted, if at all, only at the conclusion of the study." [1] There is some force to his position. How can we provide a comprehensive and conclusive definition of what religion is until we have examined and become familiar with the subject matter in depth and detail? Will not a premature definition based on insufficient evidence cause us to miss certain features of the phenomena that we may not have specified in our original formula? On the other hand, is it not true that we must have some idea of what it is we are studying in order to begin our investigation? Here then is an intriguing dilemma. It seems that we cannot know what religion is until we have studied it, and yet we cannot study it until we know what it is.

Perhaps the source of this dilemma lies in an insufficiently flexi-

---

1. Quoted in Roland Robertson, *The Sociological Interpretation of Religion,* Oxford, Blackwell, 1970, p. 34.

ble approach. It is not the case that we must begin our study knowing either nothing about the subject or knowing everything. On the contrary, we can begin with a certain common-sense knowledge of the subject in question and seek to devise scientific tools of conceptualization and investigation that will help us to learn more. Thus it is instructive to recognize that a physicist can make important discoveries in his field without defining exactly what "matter" or "physical reality" is. A biologist deals with living organisms, but often he is perplexed when asked to define exactly what "life" is. Certain entities seem to be hybrid forms that have both animate and inanimate characteristics. Are they living or dead? In a way this is a semantic question; both physicists and biologists can study these entities without deciding how the semantic problem should be resolved.

Similarly, the student of religion is often perplexed about how to classify a given phenomenon. Thus Zen is customarily called a religion, though many insist it is not a religion but a philosophy of life. Others want to say that Communism is a religion, though many people classify it as an economic or political movement. How are we to decide? In the beginning of our study of religion a certain flexibility and tentativeness in our answers are desirable. Let us look at our own customary usage and compare it with past usage and current usage among scholars in the field. The student of religion can then decide on his own operational definition that can help point out to him the area that he intends to investigate, even though he may later change and qualify this initial formula in the light of further information.

In this connection it will be helpful to glance briefly at the etymology of the word with which we are concerned. Wilfred Cantwell Smith has provided a very useful history of the word "religion" in his book *The Meaning and End of Religion.* He points out that the word is derived from the Latin *religio.* In classical antiquity the Romans performed many rituals in honor of the gods, which were functions of individual families, larger kinship groups, later of the state. A sense of obligation that a god must receive "appropriate honors" (*debitas honores*) was very strong. Smith observes:

> *The early phrase* religio mihi est *is illuminating. To say that such and such a thing was* religio *for me meant that it was mightily incumbent upon me to do it (alternatively not to do it: both are found as is not unusual with "mana," "tabu," the holy, the sacred). Oaths, family properties, cultic observances and the like were each* religio *to a man; or showing the ambivalence, one could equally say that to break a solemn oath is* religio, *that is tabu—as we might say, sacrilegious.*
>
> *Also the ritual ceremonies themselves were designated* religiones. *Throughout Latin usage right to the end of its development, the sense of rite, the outward observance of a particular practice, is to be found. This is, perhaps, related to a Roman tendency to perceive what we would call the divine or holy not so much, or not only, in the form of a figure or "god" as in that of a*

series of standardized acts. . . . The religio *of a specified god could then designate the traditional cultic pattern at his shrine.*[2]

In the first century B.C., two Roman authors use the noun *religio* to refer to some phenomenon or quality in human life that is related to earlier usage but now assumes a more universal significance. In his famous poem, *On the Nature of Things,* Lucretius takes a negative attitude toward *religio,* which he blames for "foul impieties" and inhuman acts like the human sacrifice by King Agamemnon of his daughter. Lucretius sees the task of his poem to be the freeing of mankind from the baneful power of religion—personified as a rapacious creature who shows "her head along the region skies, glowering on mortals with her hideous face."

On the other hand, Cicero takes a more positive view in his book *On the Nature of the Gods.* What Lucretius calls religion, Cicero calls superstition (*superstitio*). Cicero urges that man adopt a mean position between atheism (which is failure to honor the gods) and superstition (which is a craven and servile terror before them). Religion rather inculcates piety (*pietas*), the proper and healthy respect for the gods expressed in ritual acts of homage.

The most important event that occurs in the later history of the word in Western culture is the transformation of its meaning from a primary reference to the ritual practices of a specific cult, to a basic reference to a total system of beliefs and practices operating in a given society. The new usage already appears by implication in Patristic writings; by the time of the Reformation, several reformers, notably Calvin, refer to the "Christian religion" as a system of belief and practice which can be compared with other "religions" or systems of belief and practice. The enlightenment thinkers of the eighteenth century develop this usage further and it seems to split into three main types.

The first usage refers not to "religion," but to specific "religions." This usage is still helpful in the study of religion. Religions as specific traditions of belief, symbol, ritual practice, and ethical admonitions exist as concrete cultural forms that can be studied in the light of their historical development. Thus in this book we shall examine the influential traditions of Buddhism, Taoism, Confucianism, Judaism, Christianity, Islam, among others.

A second modern usage should be noted in order to be eschewed, so far as the scholarly study of religion is concerned. According to it there is an ideal essence of "religion" as a set of desirable beliefs and ethical standards which are then contrasted to the superstitions of most or all existing religions. The normative problem of what a good religion ought to be is a problem for philosophers, theologians, religious thinkers; however, the scholarly study of religion is rather concerned with an understanding of how religions have actually operated in human history, not with how they ought to operate according to the particular value scheme of the critic.

2. Wilfred Cantwell Smith, *The Meaning and End of Religion,* New York, Mentor Books, 1964, p. 24.

A third meaning of "religion" refers to the class of all existing religions. This usage remains as a problem and the source of a dilemma. If we refer to "religions," do we not have in mind some notion of the basis for classifying these particular systems and traditions as examples of "religion"? It is here that the question of definition still remains. Let us now consider three definitions of religion that are presently widely used by scholars to answer this question.

First of all, religion is often defined in terms of the distinction made by many "religious" people between an empirical natural order of existence and a superempirical or supernatural order of existence. Thus Roland Robertson, a contemporary sociologist, defines a religious culture as "that set of beliefs and symbols (and values deriving directly therefrom) pertaining to a distinction between an empirical and a superempirical, transcendent reality; the affairs of the empirical being subordinated to the nonempirical." He also defines "religious action" as "action shaped by an acknowledgment of the empirical/superempirical distinction."[3] Probably the majority of anthropologists and sociologists at the present time adopt some form of this position.

This definition has the advantages of exactness and specificity. It clearly delineates a certain kind of human action and symbolization —that which is oriented toward a realm above the physical natural one—and distinguishes it from other cultural acts and symbols. Furthermore, it has support in our common-sense use of the word "religion." Most of us do use the word "religion" in this way primarily to refer to beliefs in gods, spirits, and other powers who occupy a world beyond the natural one. In many ways Tyler was quite sound in suggesting long ago that the minimal definition of religion was "belief in spirits."

A second possible definition finds the presence of religion in the distinction between the sacred and profane made by most primitive societies and archaic civilizations. This definition has been expressed in classic form by Emile Durkheim in his *Elementary Forms of Religious Life*. He writes:

The real characteristic of religious phenomena is that they always suppose a bipartite division of the whole universe, known and knowable, into two classes which embrace all that exists, but which radically exclude each other. Sacred things are those which the interdictions protect and isolate; profane things, those to which these interdictions are applied and which must remain at a distance from the first. Religious beliefs are the representations which express the nature of sacred things and the relations which they sustain, either with each other or with profane things.[4]

3. Robertson, op. cit., p. 47.

4. Emile Durkheim, *The Elementary Forms of Religious Life,* London, G. Allen, 1915, p. 41.

This definition is often associated with the thesis that the basis for the sacred-profane distinction is to be found in primordial experiences characterized by feelings of awe and sacred wonder. Rudolf Otto has written a study of such experiences entitled *The Idea of the Holy.* In it Otto lists three characteristics of an experience of "the sacred" or "the holy."

First is the sense of the *tremendum* that refers to a feeling of awefulness, and *majestas* or overpowering might that includes the sense of urgency. Second, *mysterium* refers to the uncanniness and mysteriousness that also pervades the experience. Finally, there is an element of *fascinans* as the experience seems to participate in an aspiration toward some ultimate value. The prevailing affective tone thus has an ambivalent texture. The characteristics of *mysterium tremendum* have a negative effect that daunts and repels at the same time that the sense of fascination encourages a positive movement of approach and desire. Otto used the term "numinous" to specify such experiences.

Innumerable examples of the numinous can be cited from religious literature. Here are three:

> In Genesis 28:17, Jacob says, "How dreadful is this place! This is none other than the house of Elohim."

> In the Bhagavad-Gita, Chapter XI, "Seeing this thy fearful and wonderful form, O great-hearted one, the three-fold world quakes."

> In the Kena-Upanishad IV.29, "This is the way It [Brahman] is to be illustrated: What lightnings have been loosed: aaah! When that has made the eyes to be closed—aaah!—So far concerning Deity."

The ambivalence of the numinous experience can be related to two familiar words in anthropological literature. In some primitive societies, *mana* refers to power, which, although dangerous, is also desirable. Thus man moves positively toward it. In touching a sacred object in the right way and at the right time, power may be transferred to him. On the other hand, since the power is superhuman, it can also be overwhelming and destructive to man. Hence the sacred object is also *tabu,* something to be avoided, to be handled circumspectly or not handled at all.

Otto did not call the numinous an emotion, but many anthropologists have, without necessarily depending on Otto, found in intense emotional responses of this kind a definition of what is specifically religious in human culture. Thus R. H. Lowie says that the religious response is "amazement and awe; and its source is in the Supernatural, Extraordinary, Weird, Sacred, Holy, Divine." Paul Radin speaks of "a feeling of exhilaration, exaltation and awe and . . . a complete absorption in internal sensations." Alexander Goldenweiser frequently refers to a "religious thrill." [5]

5. Quoted in E. E. Evans-Pritchard, *Theories of Primitive Religion,* London, Oxford University Press, 1965, pp. 38–39.

On the other hand, it is also possible to consider the sacred as a kind of human behavior or cultural act. As Clifford Geertz observes, "the construction, apprehension, and utilization of symbolic forms are social events like any other; they are as public as marriage and as observable as agriculture." [6] Following this lead we might recognize the sacred in certain ritual acts that men perform. For example, consider this description of the plaiting of sacred mats in Tikopia rituals:

> The women . . . had to turn their bodies to the sea coast, not to the lake. . . . When the actual plaiting began a taboo of silence was imposed: the women might not speak to each other, nor the men to them. . . . All ordinary conversation was barred. Nor might the workers be approached by anyone else. A boy . . . when about to cross the maral (open space used for religious rites) was told to go inland, by the hedge, and not to go near the women.[7]

We see that in this ritual the distinction between sacred and profane reality can be recognized entirely in terms of observations of public behavior, both negative and positive. This definition has several advantages. It allows us to include under the rubric of religion a wide variety of beliefs and practices, so long as they are related to this distinction between the sacred and the ordinary. Furthermore, it can appeal to common-sense usage. Usually, we do tend to call religious any belief that is held with a sense of its sacred importance or any practice that is performed in a manner that conveys a sense of awesome and profound value.

A third definition of religion refers to the distinction between whatever is of ultimate authority and value to man and what is of penultimate or secondary importance. Thus, the theologian and philosopher Paul Tillich declares:

> Religion is the state of being grasped by an ultimate concern, a concern which qualifies all other concerns as preliminary and which itself contains the answer to the question of the meaning of our life. Therefore this concern is unconditionally serious and shows a willingness to sacrifice any finite concern which is in conflict with it.[8]

Many sociologists and anthropologists have found this notion useful and have interpreted it in terms of the society as a whole. Thus, William Lessa and Evan Vogt observe:

> Religion may be described as a system of beliefs and practices directed toward the "ultimate concern" of a society. "Ultimate

6. Clifford Geertz, "Religion as a Cultural System," in M. Banton, ed., *Anthropological Approaches to the Study of Religion*, London, Tavistock Publications, 1966, p. 5.

7. Raymond Firth, *The Work of the Gods in Tikopia*, London, Athlone Press, 1967, pp. 389–390.

8. Paul Tillich, *Christianity and the Encounter with the World Religions*, Chicago, University of Chicago Press, p. 6.

concern," a concept used by Paul Tillich, has two aspects— meaning and power. It has meaning in the sense of ultimate meaning of the central values of a society, and it has power in the sense of ultimate, sacred, or supernatural power which stands behind those values.[9]

This definition has affinities with the second one. What is ultimate and what is sacred to man seem to coalesce. This definition like the others finds support in our common-sense usage. Most societies have found it necessary not only to recommend certain rules for human behavior but to provide for these rules and practices some sort of ultimate justification or validation beyond the pragmatic fact that they are useful or are a matter of custom. The beliefs and symbols by which this ultimate validation is affirmed do tend to be called "religious" in character.

PROBLEMS IN THE
THREE DEFINITIONS

Each of these definitions is useful even though each also contains problems. For example, exceptions that we might want to call religious but which do not fit into one or the other of these definitions can be cited. Thus some phenomena that we commonly call religious do not seem, at least on one possible interpretation, to point to a transcendent or transempirical realm. Some Buddhists cultivate a state of consciousness (satori) characterized by the experience or condition of "nonduality" with this world rather than contact with a higher, transempirical world. Or again, some anthropologists have described religious rites in which a subjective experience of the sacred awe does not seem to be present. Similarly, some beliefs in a particular god or power are not connected with an ultimate justification of the norms of human behavior in that society.

Furthermore, each of these definitions reveals conceptual unclarity. The first has the advantage of definiteness and exclusivity. It specifies exactly what counts as religion (orientation toward the supernatural) and distinguishes it from what does not. For these reasons a great number of anthropologists and sociologists tend to use it as the most useful working definition of religion, preferable for their purposes to references to emotional states of sacred feeling or to ultimate values which can be vague in their application to specific phenomena.

However, the term "supernatural" or "transempirical" has one disadvantage. The word encourages us to interpret all religions according to a Western model that is far from universal. The word "supernatural" suggests a sharp division between two worlds—a natural world of physical objects and human relationships and a supernatural world of gods and supermundane realities. But such a division presupposes the recognition of a natural world that operates by strict causal laws and physical energies, which is then contrasted with a spiritual world of divine powers not subject to these laws. Such a distinction makes sense to people influenced by a sci-

9. William Lessa and Evan Vogt, eds., *A Reader in Comparative Religion*, New York, Harper & Row, 1965, p. 1.

entific culture devoted to the study of lawful regularities of the natural world. However, other cultures do not make the division in quite that way. For example, Lienhardt observes:

> I have not found it useful to adopt the distinction between "natural" and "supernatural" beings or events in order to describe the difference between men and Powers, for this distinction implies a conception of the course or laws of Nature quite foreign to Dinka thought. When, for example, the Dinka attribute lightning to a particular ultra-human power, it would falsify their understanding, and indeed exaggerate its difference from our own, to refer to a supernatural Power. The force of lightning is equally ultra-human for ourselves as for the Dinka, though the interpretation we place upon that fact is very different from theirs.[10]

The term "supernatural" seems to make the division between worlds in too radical a manner and to provide too parochial a reflection of Western oppositions between science (nature) and religion (supernatural). The same problem obtains with another proposal—"transempirical." Empirical means experiential; in the West it is closely related to scientific pursuits. Thus, "transempirical" implies a division between an empirical world open to scientific observation and a transempirical world of religion beyond its purview. The distinction has its uses; but in some cultures the gods are considered to be experienced as immediately as are other entities of the natural world.

Perhaps a better term than "supernatural" or "transempirical" to express the kind of division exhibited in many religions is the word "transcendent." This term is helpful, especially if it is used in an operational rather than substantive way. On this view, religion makes a distinction between man and something that transcends him, not substantively in the sense that the religious object is necessarily believed to occupy another world, but functionally in the sense that within his one world of experience the religious man believes that he encounters powers that are impressively greater than (transcendent to) his own.

The definition of religion in terms of the sacred has even greater difficulties. It is very difficult to distinguish a sacred emotion from other emotions of wonder and ordinary respect. Many psychologists, like William James, doubt that a distinct "religious emotion" exists. Furthermore, leading anthropologists find the distinction between sacred and profane a vague one. Thus, E. E. Evans-Pritchard observes:

> Surely . . . "sacred" and "profane" are on the same level of experience, and, far from being cut off from one another, they are so closely intermingled as to be inseparable. They cannot, therefore, either for the individual or for social activities, be put in closed departments which negate each other, one of which is left on entering the other. For instance, when some misfortune such

10. Godfrey Lienhardt, *Divinity and Experience*, Oxford, Clarendon Press, 1961, p. 29.

as sickness is believed to be due to some fault, the physical symptoms, the moral state of the sufferer, and the spiritual intervention form a unitary objective experience, and can scarcely be separated in the mind. My test of this sort of formulation is a simple one: whether it can be broken down into problems which permit testing by observation in field research, or can at least aid in a classification of observed facts. I have never found that the dichotomy of sacred and profane was of much use for either purpose.[11]

The notion of ultimacy is similarly infected with a certain vagueness. From one point of view, it could be applied to any and every justification of a behavioral norm without exception. Thus if a naturalist says that one should behave in a certain way because it enhances biological health and another says that one should do so because a god has commanded it, both have offered their own kind of ultimate justification and hence, on this view, are equally religious. But a term with such a broad width of application seems to have lost any determinate meaning.

The perplexity is engendered in part by an ambiguity in the phrase "ultimate concern." Does it refer to the mere facing of ultimate questions; to the state of being concerned about finding an answer? Or does it refer to the actual working out of a certain sort of answer? It would seem that all men and cultures exhibit "ultimate concern" in the sense that the conditions of natural existence force them to face problems about the validation of their values and norms of behavior. However, it would further seem that the solutions can vary greatly and that a distinction between a general class of religious answers and another general class of nonreligious ones ought to be made. In other words, all men probably ask limit (or ultimate) questions. They may or may not find an ultimate or religious answer.

CONCLUSION Although each of the proposed definitions has its difficulties, all of them are useful and have been adopted by influential scholars at the present time. As we have suggested, perhaps they should be treated as enunciations of specific criteria (transcendence, sacredness, ultimacy) that operate in our use of the word "religion." These criteria are not mutually exclusive. Rather they complement one another and together point out an area of human activity and concern which is distinctive and has played an important part in human culture. The definitions are not definitive descriptions of a universal essence but they are "pointers" that designate in a general way a kind of human activity that is recognizable and worth our attention. The task is to use some or all of these criteria to fashion a working definition of religion that helps the student of religion explore aspects of human behavior that he finds worthy of investigation. The more specific definition will usually include other factors in addition

11. Evans-Pritchard, op. cit., p. 65.

to the formal criteria. For example, Clifford Geertz in an important article emphasizes symbolic activity. He defines religion as:

> (1) *a system of symbols which acts to* (2) *establish powerful, pervasive, and long-lasting moods and motivations in men by* (3) *formulating conceptions of a general order of existence and* (4) *clothing these conceptions with such an aura of factuality that* (5) *the moods and motivations seem uniquely realistic.*[12]

Another anthropologist, Anthony Wallace, emphasizes ritual behavior and defines religion as "a set of rituals, rationalized by myth, which mobilizes supernatural powers for the purpose of achieving or preventing transformations of state in man and nature." [13]

The beginning student of religion is thus advised to approach the problem of definition in an open, flexible manner. The question of the definition of religion is not the question of a fact that is either so or not so. It is the question of a choice about how to use a word, and this depends on the purposes and concerns of the prospective user. Shakespeare long ago asked: "What's in a name? That which we call a rose/By any other name would smell as sweet." Humpty Dumpty in Lewis Carroll's *Through the Looking Glass* noted, "When *I* use a word it means just what I choose it to mean—neither more or less." When Alice asked whether you can make words mean so many different things, Humpty Dumpty answered, "The question is which is to be master—that's all."

Let the beginning student consider the criteria that operate in his own usage and compare them with the definitions proposed by leading scholars in the field. He can then decide on an operational definition that seems to be of most use to him at the start of his studies, but which will be held in a tentative manner open to correction and qualification in the light of his increasing familiarization with the field.

12. Geertz, op. cit., p. 4.
13. Anthony Wallace, *Religion: An Anthropological View*, New York, Random House, 1966, p. 107.

RELIGION
AS ACTION
AND MEANING:
RITUAL AND MYTH

In the first chapter we observed that the most useful way to study religion is in terms of actions and meanings, in terms of what people do and how they symbolize what they do. We now turn to some concrete examples of how such study is performed. We shall consider some specific questions that are generated by the methodological perspectives we have noted. In this brief survey we shall not adopt the position of any one school or single investigator but attempt to show how the various perspectives interact with one another to provide a helpful understanding of religious action.

Let us begin by looking at a specific example of religion in action in a primitive society.

TIKOPIA:
THE RITUAL OF
THE "HOT FOOD"

Tikopia is a small island in the British Solomon Islands Protectorate. A sequence of rituals called "the Work of the Gods" was performed there regularly at seasonal intervals until 1956, when the conversion to Christianity of the major chief caused their abandonment. The time of the rites was determined mainly by seasonal changes; one part of the rites was performed roughly in April, when the winds settled down to blow steadily from the southeast or east-southeast and continued thus for about six months. A second part of the series took place around October, when these trade winds were replaced with normally light winds alternating with flat calms.

The series as a whole was elaborate and took weeks to perform. The sequence included a symbolic fire ritual to initiate the cycle; a resacralization of canoes; a reconsecration of temples; a series of planting and harvest rites for the yam; a sacred dance festival; several memorial rites on the sites of vanished temples; and the ritual manufacture of a pigment called tumeric, which is extracted from the root of a plant.

Four clans, politically autonomous and each under its own chief, participated in the rituals in which one chief, the Arika Kafika, occupied a role of special prestige as a kind of *primus inter pares,* i.e., the first among equals.

As an example of the entire sequence, let us consider more closely one of these rites—the ritual of the "hot food"—as it is described by the anthropologist Raymond Firth in *The Work of the Gods in Tikopia.*[1] In preparation for this particular rite, yams are first cooked in the oven house. Shortly before noon, the oven is uncovered, the food is removed and put in a shallow wooden dish of unique shape. The dish is carried to the main building and set in a ritual position in an area devoted to the gods on the seaward side close to the center post.

Meanwhile, the participants in the room prepare for the ceremony by each taking a large leaf in his hand. "An air of tense expectation" grips the crowd and speech is only in whispers. Finally, a basket of yam tubers, smoking hot from the oven, is brought in, and the bearer quickly distributes them to the members. Each man catches his hot yam deftly in his leaf-covered hands and bites it as quickly as he can, while it is still hot. The first person to successfully swallow a mouthful of the scalding food makes a sucking noise with his lips. This man is considered to be specially favored from that time forth. "Ku tu i te Atua," i.e., "He stands in with the god," it is afterward said.

The Arika Kafika, the chief of the most prestigious tribe, then seats himself before the wooden dish of food devoted to the gods. A libation made from the kava plant is served. The chief, without turning his head, takes the cup and, making obeisance by raising it to his forehead, pours it out in front of him. This is done four times in honor of various gods believed to be present. After this, the chief returns to his former seat. The two yams in the special dish are divided, one given away as an ordinary food portion, the other laid in a small basket belonging to the chief.

As soon as the rites are over, the tension relaxes. "The kava of gods is finished," someone says. People begin to talk of their experiences, how their lips burned, how tears came to their eyes, how they made puffing noises in an effort to cool off the burning portions. One who clumsily dropped his yam is laughed at in good-natured fashion by the others. These jovial exchanges are in sharp contrast to the earlier attitudes of respect and restraint exhibited during the ceremony. What is the meaning of this behavior? According to Firth, a kind of "elementary communion feast" has taken place. The feeling of awe is generated by the belief that the highest

1. Raymond Firth, *The Work of the Gods in Tikopia,* New York, Athlone Press, 1967, hereinafter *Work.*

A Tikopia aristocrat. (From Raymond Firth, We the Tikopia; *courtesy of George Allen & Unwin, Ltd.)*

god, Atua i Kafika, has been directly present at the ceremony in the person of the chief. Thus the Arika made the following statement to Firth: "I who have sat there am him [the God]; he does not eat since he has left his kava [a libation] to be made by the brethren [the family of principal clan gods]. I there am the God; he has come to me, because I am the chief of importance. From olden times the Arika Kafika has been the chief of prime importance since he has been rendered so by the God." [2]

It is believed that the rite was instituted by the Atua i Kafika when he lived on earth long ago. Since the Atua ate only hot food, he wanted a ceremony to follow his personal habits, and "to this day he himself attends the rite to observe that it is duly carried out."

So much, then, for the rite and the most immediate explanation of its significance. Can anything further be said about its meaning and general import for the life of the Tikopia?

2. *Work*, p. 157.

This account has introduced us to the exceedingly important human behavioral pattern called *ritual*. Ritual is so pervasive and significant in human culture as a whole and in religion in particular that neither can be adequately understood without considering it in some detail. Ritual has been defined as "the formal acting out of a ceremony, usually repeated in exactly the same way on specified occasions." [3] This definition stresses two important features of ritual: the pronounced *formality* of the action and its *repetition* at regular intervals. However, the word "ceremony" must be interpreted in a broad sense to include both elaborate public rites and those simpler gestures that occur between small social units, as when the members of a family regularly bow to each other before eating the evening meal, or two friends shake hands on meeting. Again, we may tend to associate rituals with sacred occasions involving reference to gods and the supernatural world; but we should also recognize that secular, or nonreligious, rituals are possible as when, for example, a culture hero is remembered and celebrated by the community at regular intervals through formal recitations and other symbolic acts.

RITUAL AND MYTH

The question of why men perform ritual acts like those of the Tikopia cycle is a significant one. These rituals involve many behavioral elements that in themselves are not puzzling. In the ritual of the "hot food," men gather together to eat yams. Both the act of eating and the social context in which it is performed are intelligible acts for human beings, who need nourishment and social conviviality. But why the formalization of the actions, the insistence on exact procedural sequences, the air of solemnity, the sense of awe that at times overcomes the participants, the behavioral reference to realities not immediately apparent to the physical senses? Is there any point to such behavior; can we make sense of it and put it into some kind of intelligible pattern that will establish its human appropriateness and reasonableness?

We have already noted how the Tikopia answer this question in terms of a *myth*. According to them, the rite of the "hot food" was set up by Atua i Kafika, the principal deity of Tikopia, while he still lived on earth. Since he ate only hot food, the rite is faithful to his habits.

The word "myth" is derived from the Greek word *mythos*, which literally means "story" and was originally used to refer to the many stories of the gods found in Greek religion. However, in the history of Western culture, many philosophers and theologians have rejected the mythos of Greek religion; the former in the name of rational "logos" or philosophical thought; the latter in the name of the Christian faith. As a result, the word "myth" has become associated in the West with a set of pejorative connotations and is in popular speech almost a synonym for "untrue," "false," or "absurdly fantastic."

However, such judgments prevent a careful description of the

3. Ralph Ross, *Symbols and Civilization,* New York, Harcourt Brace Jovanovich, 1957, p. 182.

data unobscured by premature judgments and emotional denunciations. Investigators of culture find that they still need a word like myth, not to express a negative value judgment about the absurdity or falsity of the material, but to classify a kind of story that appears in a variety of societies with distinctive characteristics worthy of notice. In this book, "myth" is used as a category of *objective* classification of a certain kind of sacred story that can be found in various cultures. No negative valuation of these stories is implied by the term, which should be disinfected of such connotations. Thus Bronislaw Malinowski argues:

> *There exists a special class of stories, regarded as sacred, embodied in ritual, morals, and social organization, and which form an integral and active part of primitive culture. These stories live not by idle interest, not as fictitious or even as true narratives, but are to the natives a statement of a primeval, greater, and more relevant reality, by which the present life, fates, and activities of mankind are determined, the knowledge of which supplies men with the motive for ritual and moral actions, as well as with indications as to how to perform them.*[4]

For example, Malinowski goes on to point out that the Trobrianders make important distinctions between the kinds of stories that they tell. First are folk tales (*kukwanebu*), which are often of a fantastic and grotesque nature, told for pleasure without implication that they are necessarily true, sacred, or important. In this class are stories of hostile snakes slain by young heroes; ogres that afflict villagers; the rivalry existing between various animals and insects. This is the world of fairy tales, personal dreams, wish fulfillment, fantasies, vicarious adventures.

A second group of stories are called *libwogwo*. These stories recount the actual experiences of the teller and are believed to be true; the information they impart is deemed relevant and important to the hearers.

But finally, there is a third class of stories called by the natives *liliu*. These are the sacred tales or myths which are in many respects very different from the others. "If the first class are told for amusement, the second to make a serious statement and satisfy social ambition, the third are regarded, not merely as true, but as venerable and sacred . . . The *myth* comes into play when rite, ceremony, or a social or moral rule demands justification, warrant of antiquity, reality, and sanctity." [5]

In general, myths are stories about events which happened long ago and which provide the normative model, the paradigm or archetypal pattern, for some human condition or custom. Mircea Eliade observes:

> *Speaking for myself, the definition that seems least inadequate because most embracing is this: Myth narrates a sacred history;*

4. Bronislaw Malinowski, *Magic, Science and Religion*, Garden City, N.Y., Doubleday Anchor Books, 1954, p. 108.
5. Ibid., p. 107.

*it relates an event that took place in primordial time, the fabled
time of the "beginnings." In other words, myth tells how, through
the deeds of supernatural Beings, a reality came into existence,
be it the whole of reality, the Cosmos, or only a fragment of
reality—an island, a species of plant, a particular kind of human
behavior, an institution. Myth, then, is always an account of a
"creation"; it related how something was produced, began to be.*[6]

Myths concerned with "origins" and "beginnings" could then be
appropriately called etiological in function, but the sense in which
this is meant should be carefully distinguished from the etiological
explanations of a modern scientist, who may also be interested in
the "origins" of the solar system or perhaps in the "beginnings" of
life on earth according to evolutionary theory.

Although tribal myths also are concerned with origins and include
stories about how various natural phenomena came into being, it is
a serious confusion to think of them as similar in intention though
inferior in value to our modern scientific explanations. The scientific
cosmologies are interested in determining the exact sequential series of empirical changes leading from a past to a present state of
the natural universe; the tribal myth is, rather, concerned with the
validation of some present human circumstance by relating it to a
primordial sacred event which is both its ultimate cause and its justification.

Even though we may grant that some inevitable overlapping and
confusion may occur between a mythic and a scientific account of
"origins," the fact remains that the profound differences in the
mode of discourse and in the basic categories of relevance and intention render them not so much rival accounts of the same phenomena, as entirely different realms of discourse with very different
concerns and intentions. Myth, properly understood, is not an early
attempt to do what modern science can now do better, any more
than a poem is an early attempt to express what a geometrical
theorem and proof can state more clearly and convincingly.

We will return to this point when we consider more closely the
expressive function of myth. For the moment, let us consider a typical tribal myth of the Trobrianders, as summarized by Malinowski.
According to the natives of the village of Laba'i, people originally
lived very differently from the way they do at present. They lived un-
derground in a more sacred region where they possessed the
power of rejuvenation by sloughing off their old skin, like a snake,
at regular intervals. It is to this region that man presumably returns
after death.

Present-day social life in this particular village of Laba'i began
when representatives of the four main clans emerged to the surface
of the earth, one after another, from a hole in the ground. Following
them came the animals associated with each clan; first the iguana,
then the dog, the pig, and finally the crocodile. Then occurred an
apparently trivial event. The dog and pig ran around, and the dog,

6. Mircea Eliade, *Myth and Reality*, trans. W. Trask, New York, Harper &
Row, 1963, pp. 5–6.

seeing the fruit of the *noku* plant, nosed it, and finally ate it. Said the pig: "Thou eatest *noku,* thou eatest dirt; thou art low-bred, a commoner; the chief, the guya'u, shall be I." Ever since then the chiefs of the Pig clan have been the most important leaders. Malinowski observes:

> To understand this myth, you must have a good knowledge of their sociology, religion, customs, and outlook. Then and only then, can you appreciate what this story means to the natives and how it can live in their life. If you stayed among them and learned the language you would constantly find it active in discussion and squabbles in reference to the relative superiority of the various clans and in the discussions about the various food taboos which frequently raise fine questions of casuistry. Above all, if you were brought into contact with communities where the historical process of the spread of influence of the Malasi clan is still in evolution, you would be brought face to face with this myth as an active force.[7]

THE THEORY OF THE RITUAL BASIS OF MYTH

As we have already noted, myths are usually associated with rituals. The precise nature of this "association" has exercised a good deal of attention from scholars. An interesting theory has been advanced that ritual and myth exhibit an essential correlation, so that a sacred myth in a culture will always be found to be the expression or oral interpretation of a ritual. In an extreme form, not usually propounded by its more judicious expositors, the theory suggests that ritual always precedes myth in a causal nexus, so that genuine myths are to be considered as the verbal articulation of certain primal ritual acts of the given culture.

In this extreme form the theory has not found acceptance, for a number of reasons. Significant myths that cannot easily be attached to a ritual are recognizable in many cultures; also, there are notable examples where rituals have been fashioned to conform to a new myth. Furthermore, the thesis in its radical causal form seems to be involved in the unresolvable and unnecessary chicken-egg kind of dilemma. We cannot find an empirically verifiable period in human culture where only ritual existed without myth; we rather discover in all existing cultures the two in dynamic interaction. Why, then, make the unnecessary and unsubstantiated hypothesis that one is the temporal basis of the other? Finally, the theory seems to gain its force from a priori stipulation rather than empirical investigation. By definition, I can declare that only those stories associated with rituals are "genuine or authentic myths." Other impressive stories of a sacred nature not so related are then excluded by fiat from inclusion under this rubric. Yet the stories so summarily dismissed may in all other respects possess the characteristics and functions of myths in that culture. A more judicious statement is provided by Clyde Kluckhohn when he observes:

7. Malinowski, op. cit., p. 113.

The facts do not permit any universal generalizations as to ritual being the "cause" of myth or vice versa. Their relationship is rather that of intricate mutual interdependence, differently structured in different cultures and probably at different times in the same culture.[8]

It is significant that Kluckhohn's careful modification of the ritual-myth theory still retains the sense of an "intricate interdependence" because this is the basic insight which the theory has sought to convey. Too often, ritual has been thought of as purely secondary phenomenon, a kind of symbolic representation of a meaning that is already clear and complete in the ideational form of a belief or dogma. The ritual is then seen as a gratuitous gesture which could be eliminated, if necessary, without serious loss. The insight that must be restored and preserved is that if the myth is an explanation of the ritual, it is also true that the ritual is a kind of explanation or embodiment of the myth, so that the teaching in word and story is only truly fulfilled by its ritual counterpart and base.

Ritual is an element of religion and culture that needs to be emphasized, even at the risk of exaggeration, since the opposite error of underestimating its importance is more serious. Yet ritual is the element most likely to be neglected by Western intellectuals, who naturally are strongly influenced by the ideational elements in culture and life. Thus, in considering a phenomenon like religion, the tendency is first to stress the thought content of religion and to ask questions concerning the "beliefs" of a given people or religious group. Even when a broader set of experiences causes us to enlarge our categories somewhat to include more *concrete* ideational elements like myths and other imagery, we still tend to conceive of a religious stance as the adherence to one or the other of these ideational elements. What myths do they believe? we may still wonder, hoping thereby to determine the essential character of a people's religious approach to existence. The emphasis on ritual helps us to see that action, behavior, operational deeds, are as important, perhaps more important, than solely ideational factors in determining a religious stance.

In this connection, R. R. Marett argues that "savage religion is something not so much thought out as danced out; . . . in other words, it develops under conditions, psychological and sociological, which favor emotional and motor processes, whereas ideation remains relatively in abeyance."[9] Although Marett is usually interpreted as having overstressed the subjectively emotional aspect of religion, it is significant that in this passage he rather emphasizes the "motor" activities of the body itself. The emphasis on ritual is related to this point. The body itself, with its various postures and

An Alaskan "yake," or carved wooden figure, used by a shaman in certain ritual dances. (Courtesy of the American Museum of Natural History.)

8. Clyde Kluckhohn, "Myths and Ritual: A General Theory," in William Lessa and Evan Vogt, eds., *A Reader in Comparative Religion,* New York, Harper & Row, 1965, p. 148.

9. R. R. Marett, *The Threshold of Religion,* London, Methuen, 1909, p. xxi.

stances, is itself a vehicle of symbolic communication. The body conveys meaning as well as words and ideas.

At the very least, then, we can see how ritual action can support and reinforce the ideational meanings of myth and dogma. However, we can go further and observe, as is evidently the intent of those stressing the ritual foundation of religion, and insist that the ritual may bear and convey meanings only partially converted into an ideational form. In other words, it is a serious mistake to think of the ritual as the symbolic dramatic enactment of a meaning already clearly expressed in some kind of ideational mode. On the contrary, the ritual may give a depth of significance and vital power to the religious intention which the accompanying myth itself needs for the full apprehension of its meaning.

Indeed, an emphasis on ritual will also help us to avoid an intellectualistic distortion of our understanding of myth itself. We must remember that myth itself in a tribal society is not a story read in solitude and apprehended by the inner mind. Myth is first of all the product of an oral society where stories are not written and read, but memorized and uttered aloud to a communal group. Myth is therefore itself a ritual act, something that is uttered, an oral event taking place within the environs of a living society. Myth is essentially a social transaction; something is proclaimed and something is heard; the full meaning of the myth includes the tones and overtones in which it is delivered, the total context in which it is listened to.

All this is not to revert to the theory of the ritual basis of myth which we have already rejected in its radical form. But the recognition of the dramatic behavioral, indeed, bodily dimension of religious behavior must not thereby be denied. The religious stance maintains at its center *acts* involving the total person; thought and idea are important only when they participate in the total behavioral situation. Any analysis of religion neglecting or obscuring this important insight does serious violence and distortion to the phenomenon it is purporting to describe. As Anthony Wallace puts it:

The primary phenomenon of religion is ritual. Ritual is religion in action; it is the cutting edge of the tool. Belief, although its recitation may be a part of the ritual, or a ritual in its own right, serves to explain, to rationalize, to interpret and direct the energy of the ritual performance. It is not a question of priority in time . . . in observed human behavior the two phenomena go together; few if any rituals are any longer instituted before a mythic base is invented to account for them. The primacy is instrumental: just as the blade of the knife has instrumental priority over the handle, and the barrel of a gun over the stock, so does the ritual have instrumental priority over myth. It is ritual which accomplishes what religion sets out to do.[10]

10. Anthony Wallace, *Religion: An Anthropological View,* New York, Random House, 1966, p. 102.

In the last section we raised the question why human beings should
perform rituals, since rituals do not seem to possess an immediately practical biological purpose in the same sense as an act like
hunting or sleeping. Yet men in all cultures overlay practical activities like eating, for example, with ritual patterns of behavior.
Why do they do so?

THE FUNCTIONAL
THEORY OF RITUAL

We have already noted that in tribal societies the participants
themselves put the answer in mythic terms. Thus, myth justifies for
Tikopia the rite of the hot food in the sense that a god is declared
to have commanded it. Myth also explains some of the specific elements of the ritual; hot yams are eaten because it is said that the
god, long ago when he lived on earth, had such eating habits. If we
ask why the Tikopia cycle as a whole was performed, the answer of
the Tikopia, as summarized by Firth, is that the ceremonies are the
means

> of maintaining contact with powerful spiritual beings and inducing
> them to look with favor upon Tikopia by the grant of food and
> health. The spiritual beings were conceived as being in reciprocal
> relationship with the leaders of particular lineages and clans. . . .
> Contact with them was to be maintained partly on the same pat-
> tern as contact with powerful human beings, that is, by presenta-
> tion of gifts and conduct of abasement. But they had to be treated
> with even more deference and even more formality. In particular,
> they had to be addressed by special titles not necessarily known
> to ordinary men and in much more elaborate set phraseology.[11]

Such is an interpretation as provided in the forms of thought
familiar to the participants themselves. Sociologists and anthropologists have evolved another set of interpretative categories that
suggest that rituals may continue to be enacted by a people for
reasons other than those explicitly stated in the given mythic explanation. This approach has led to an impressive analysis which has
come to be known as *functional theory*. According to it, religious
rites and beliefs perform certain positive functions related to social
or personal problems that cause the participants to adhere to them,
whether or not they are consciously aware of the full effect and importance of these effects.

This suggestion presupposes that human action is complex and
ambiguous, and reveals both conscious and unconscious dimensions in which different sets of motivation apply. A person or a social group may perform an action with a certain goal in mind, but
really value and reinforce the act for other purposes.

The sociologist Robert Merton has helped clarify the semantic difficulties involved in this point by distinguishing between manifest
and latent functions. Manifest functions are the purposes of an act
as the actors themselves understand and express them; the latent
functions are the results of the act which are unknown to or neglected by the actors but which determine the real value of the act
and the need for its repetition. The manifest functions are observed

11. *Work*, p. 6.

by the participants themselves, but the latent ones are more likely to be perceived by objective observers. Thus, while the participants in a primitive ritual may offer a manifestly mythic explanation of their action, the modern sociologist and anthropologist believes he can discern latent functional results of the action of a different sort. We can summarize these latent functional aspects under three headings: social, biological-psychological, and depth-psychological.

THE SOCIAL
FUNCTION OF
RELIGION

Sufficient examples of how ritual contributes to social integration have already been given and the point is fairly obvious and incontrovertible. A human society is a complex whole made up of many subordinate parts—sexes, age groupings, professional and economic classes, political bodies. In a biological organism, the various parts are integrated into a working, functioning whole according to innate biological patterns automatically establishing and maintaining the very possibility of the life and being of that organism. So much differentiation and relative freedom among the parts of human society is possible that their integration into a common whole seems constantly threatened. One way of overcoming this threat toward disintegration and dissolution of the social bonds is by means of communal rites and rituals.

Ritual-myth complexes accomplish this social integrative function in at least six ways.

1. First is their assistance in the *symbolic articulation* of the social patterns and relationships themselves. Even a cursory examination of primitive myth and ritual must impress the mind with the remarkable congruence of mythic patterns with the specific social patterns of the group in question. Such resemblances are not occasional, but pervasive, perhaps universal, and easy to detect. Often the complex hierarchy of gods and spirits in a given culture will almost exactly correspond to the hierarchy of social segments. In Tikopia, the "religious pyramid of the gods" exactly corresponds to the pyramids of social relation existing among the clans. The chief god, Atua i Kafika, is specially worshiped by the Kafika clan, though the other clans acknowledge him in addition to their own special clan gods. By the same token, the Kafika clan has a very real though legally undefined position of special prestige among the clans. The hierarchy of gods thus provides a perfectly adequate symbolic articulation of this social reality.

Furthermore, in the rituals, the Arika Kafika, head of the most prestigious clan, is given special functions of honor. For example, he declares the beginning of "the Work of the Gods" and has the leading place in the opening rite of the firebrands. On the other hand, he is in no sense an autocrat or absolute monarch over the other tribes. So, in various rituals, each tribe and its chief will in turn occupy a place of special importance and honor. In this manner, the subtle relationships existing between the tribes are expressed in myth and ritual.

2. A second social function is even more important. Something in man's complex social and axiological make-up is not content with

the mere recognition of a social situation as a brute fact, but requires for it some kind of justification. Myth and ritual meet this need in a striking, if obvious, fashion. By relating the human world to a world of divine forces and powers, the social milieu receives a kind of *validation* it does not seem to possess when considered in its own right alone.

3. A third social function is a *performatory* one. It is one thing to state and articulate a certain relationship among the parts of a social group. In the ritual, the relationship is acted out, performed, realized, made to occur. This point may be circular, but it is no less valid for that. Ritual accomplishes social integration by an act of social integration. By coming together in an integral act, the society discovers that it has been maintained, preserved, and reinforced as an integral entity. The family that prays together stays together because in doing their religious thing together they are together.

4. A fourth social function is less obvious but very important. Ritual performs a *heuristic* function. It assists us in concentrating attention and focusing energies in such a way that our human capacities cooperate at their most potent level in the performance of a desired act. As Mary Douglas observes: "an external symbol can mysteriously help the co-ordination of brain and body." Thus:

> The Dinka herdsman hurrying home to supper, knots a bundle of grass at the wayside, a symbol of delay. Thus he expresses outwardly his wish that the cooking may be delayed for his return. The rite holds no magic promise that he will now be in time for supper. He does not then dawdle home thinking that the action will itself be effective. He redoubles his haste. His action has not wasted time, for it has sharpened the focus of his attention on his wish to be in time.[12]

5. Ritual can also provide a directly creative function in solving personal and social dilemmas. It can help man to solve difficulties, release tensions, resolve ambiguities in his social relationships that otherwise might fester and eventually break the social bond.

Too often, functional analysis has presented its thesis in too static a manner, as if a human society were already determined in all its social details and the ritual existed simply to affirm and maintain the already fixed relationship. In point of fact, even the most traditional and unchanging society has dynamic elements within it. Peoples and groups, and the relations among them, are constantly changing. In ritual celebrations, the status of a given leader or clan is either *reaffirmed* or perhaps slightly *modified* according to the slight changes that may be introduced into the ritual each time.

Thus, Firth emphasizes that although the general shape of the Tikopia cycle was fixed, room for innovation and modification was also evident. He concludes:

> In such ways ritual not only represents, describes, and maintains the social order; it may also help in the formation and develop-

12. Mary Douglas, *Purity and Danger*, New York, Praeger, 1966, pp. 63–64.

*ment of the social order. It can have an adaptive and even crea-
tive function. By giving occasion for the public assumption of
roles it also gives occasion for interpreting and modifying them,
and so for re-shaping the social order. But as it does these
things, by the very messages of status-involvement and exercise
of initiative that it conveys it may also be a source of competition
and disunity; one man's ritual asset may become another man's
social affront.*[13]

6. Finally, we can observe in ritual and myth a *mitigative* function
that is subtle but probably of great value in promoting social unity.
It might be wondered why the facts of social relationship cannot be
said in a clear and unequivocal manner without the indirection of
ritual and myth. Such a question indicates no doubt the commenda-
ble honesty of the asker, but also, perhaps, his lack of sensitivity to
human feeling. As Confucius long ago noted, ritual serves as a
buffer protecting the delicate egos of the participants while ena-
bling unpleasant actualities, such as the ascendancy of one man
over another, to be stated in a way that is palatable and acceptable
to both. The blunt edge of the truth is softened by the pleasing
complexity of the ritual. As Firth points out, "statements" can be
made through ritual "in a manner less brusque, more protracted,
more behaviorally involved, than with ordinary language." Thus:

*One can assume that every individual has emotional dispositions
and tensions arising from his relation to the external world, including members of his own society. . . . What ritual has done is
to provide routinization and canalization for such tensions. These
are not left for random expression, but are assigned their time
and place for explicit mention and acting-out.*[14]

THE BIOLOGICAL-
PSYCHOLOGICAL
FUNCTION
OF RELIGION

A second major area where the functionality of ritual can be observed is what is here called the psychological-biological. This hy-
phenated term points to the human area where personal and biological problems centering around birth, maturation, and sexual life
are intertwined. These experiences lead to the question of personal
identity. The person must discover who he is in the sense that he
must work out a behavioral style appropriate to his being as a child,
an adult, a boy, a girl, a man, a woman. The question of identity
may also assume a more profound "metaphysical" aspect as he
seeks to determine his "ultimate" nature and destiny in the universe. However, in the interests of analytical clarity, we wish here to
separate this deeper question of identity from the question of identity as a psychological-biological organism which in this section is
our concern.

An intriguing and vivid example of the assistance of myth in this
problem of forming personal identity is to be found in the popular
Trickster stories of the North American Indians. For example, ac-

13. *Work*, p. 23.
14. Ibid., pp. 25, 23.

cording to one story Trickster is butchering a buffalo. He is using a knife with his right hand, when his left arm suddenly grabs the buffalo. The right arm speaks out: "Give that back to me. It is mine!" The left arm releases its hold but shortly afterwards grabs hold of the right arm; a vicious fight between the arms follows and the left arm is wounded.

In another story Trickster treats his anus as if it were an independent agent. After killing some ducks, Trickster tells his anus to keep watch over them while he sleeps. Some foxes then draw near but, much to their surprise, they are startled by the sound of expelled gas. They are frightened by this sound several times, but finally gain courage enough to approach the sleeping Trickster and eat the ducks. When Trickster awakes, he is angry with his anus for doing such a poor job as a guard. He takes a piece of burning wood and burns the mouth of his own anus in punishment. This act causes him to cry out in pain.

What do these strange stories mean? As Mary Douglas points out:

> The trickster starts as an unselfconscious, amorphous being. As the story unfolds he gradually discovers his own identity, gradually recognizes and controls his own anatomical parts; he oscillates between female and male, but eventually fixes his own male sexual role; and finally learns to assess his environment for what it is. . . . Trickster begins, isolated, amoral and unselfconscious, clumsy, ineffectual, an animal-like buffoon. Various episodes prune down and place more correctly his bodily organs so that he ends by looking like a man. At the same time he begins to have a more consistent set of social relations and to learn hard lessons about his physical environment. In one important episode he mistakes a tree for a man and responds to it as he would to a person until eventually he discovers it is a mere inanimate thing. So gradually he learns the functions and limits of his being.[15]

Innumerable myths about young heroes who slay monsters, rescue maidens, find hidden treasures and finally solve fundamental problems for their society no doubt reflect this process of human growth and achievement of personal and social identity. Rituals also participate in this process.

Probably the most significant rituals in any culture are those having to do with rites of initiation, the most important of which mark the transition from youthful existence to that of full participation in all the privileges and responsibilities of the adult members of the community. These rites are both civil and religious in character, since the initiant is usually introduced to the full extent of his social responsibilities and to the deeper meaning of the religious lore of his tribe. Many kinds of initiation rites exist; some are for women,

INITIATION RITUALS

15. Douglas, op. cit., pp. 79–80.

some are for entrance into special societies within the larger society as a whole. However, the most important and extensive ones concern the transition of the male from his state of childhood to full manhood in the tribe.

The following account of an initiation rite, by H. Ian Hogbin, in a New Guinea village conveys some of the qualities of the initiation ceremony in a vivid form. Hogbin tells how the villagers selected two old men to be guardians. A large building was erected in the bush to house the boys. The guardians told the boys that during the next few months they would be tested to see whether they were fit to be presented as a sacrificial meal for the monsters. If they were worthy they would pass through whole and be evacuated. But anyone who failed to measure up to the requirements would remain fast in the monster's belly and never be heard of again. For about three months the boys waited in the house and were subject to beatings, forced to stay awake for long periods, and took only a minimum amount of food and drink.

> At length the day arrived for the summoning of the monsters. Word had been sent out to the villages which had proclaimed the taboo, and a vast concourse of people was by this time in attendance. They remained till the last rite ended, causing severe strain on their hosts' resources.
>
> The pretence was that the monsters lived underground and a hole was accordingly dug from which they could emerge. At first only a faint humming was heard, and the women murmured amongst themselves that the tree roots must be scraping their flanks. Soon afterwards a man covered with earth went along to the village to announce how deep down the monsters had been but that they had at last appeared. The humming now became louder, till in the end the whole countryside rang with the booming of dozens of bullroarers.
>
> The boys had to listen for a few days and were then brought out and shown by their guardians, with much impressive ritual, how the noise was made. A poisonous fish was later flourished in front of their mouths, and they were warned that if a word of what had been disclosed crossed their lips they would perish as assuredly as if they had swallowed a deadly toxin.
>
> This revelation was followed by the incision rite. This time the boys were cut by one or other of the guardians, but on all subsequent occasions each person operated on himself. A long low shed had been built to represent one of the monsters, and inside the two men waited with their obsidian knives. The lads were taken in turn, each one being carried on the back of his sponsor, who also served as a support while the gash was being made. The blood, as the first which they had shed, was especially sacred, and the sponsors gathered it in leaves for use later as face paint.[16]

16. H. Ian Hogbin, "Pagan Religion in a New Guinea Village," in John Middleton, ed., *Gods and Rituals*, New York, Natural History Press, 1967, pp. 57–61.

Afterwards the youths were given a ceremonial bath by their sponsors. This was followed by a great feast where the boys sat while relatives and friends danced and sang songs in their honor.

In his classic account of initiation rites, Arnold Van Gennep characterizes them as "rites of passage" in which, by "crossing a threshold," the initiate feels that he has moved from one world to another. The basic pattern is separation from a previous world, transition, incorporation into the new world.[17] The separation and transition are a period of isolation and danger, as when the New Guinea youth are physically isolated inside the house, tormented by the threat of monsters, and finally wounded by the incision rite, in such a way that the possibility of death becomes very real. Afterward, they are incorporated into a new social reality in the manner indicated. In this example the transition is presented mainly on the social level, but the model is also used to elaborate a more inner rite of passage from a mundane to a sacred mode of spiritual being. Through the dark night of the soul the descent into the belly of the primeval monster, the symbolic death, the resurrection to a new mode of being, the initiate is transformed, re-created, reestablished as a new being.

In the history of religions many examples of this initiation pattern can be recognized; religious art, myths, and theologies constantly exhibit this model, and it is one of the basic and most convincing examples of how ritual provides the structural base for the ideational themes and flights of imagery in a religion's symbolic system.

At the moment, however, we are concerned in particular with how initiation rites provide the means by which the initiate works out the task of forming both his personal and social identity. Various psychological interpretations of initiation patterns overlap and complement rather than contradict one another. For example, circumcision and subincision rites among primitive tribes can be interpreted according to functional theory as the means whereby fear is faced and overcome through the endurance of the frightening act. Anthropologists influenced by Freud will further observe that the perennial hostilities between fathers and sons are also faced and resolved through an act in which a real threat by the "father" is transformed into a symbolic act that resolves tensions and unites the fathers and sons in a common bond.[18] Bruno Bettelheim, on the other hand, argues that in the subincision rite the male discovers a means whereby he works out the problem of his relationship and identity, not in terms of the father and male, but in terms of the mother and the female. The envy of the male for the woman, who possesses a strange power through her menstrual cycle, is mitigated by a rite in which the male also bleeds, thus imitating the woman and finding compensation for his own "inferiority" in this respect.[19]

17. Arnold Van Gennep, *Rites of Passage,* Chicago, The University of Chicago Press, 1960, pp. 20–21.

18. Geza Roheim, *The Eternal Ones of the Dream: A Psychoanalytic Interpretation of Australian Myth and Ritual,* New York, International Universities Press, 1945.

19. Bruno Bettelheim, *Symbolic Wounds,* New York, Collier Books, 1962.

Such practices play an important part in the concerns of the tribal religion. The sexual nature of man is a fact of his life that no philosophy or religion of any scope has ignored. Tribal man has found the means, through ritual and symbol, to resolve tensions and psychic conflicts, restore inner equilibrium, and provide a sense of social, personal, and sexual identity for the developing and maturing person. Indeed, a sophisticated modern who has rejected all myth and ritual as barbaric superstition must still face the task of fashioning a self-image and style with which and by which he can live. Scorning the symbolic tools of a religious culture, the modern often finds himself on a psychologist's couch instead, where he works out a personality transformation (a rite of passage) through myths and symbols (now called dream imagery), in ways similar to those practiced by the primitive religionist on a less deliberate and more traditional level.

THE DEPTH-
PSYCHOLOGICAL
FUNCTION OF
RELIGION

The functions of religion so far noted are interesting and important. However, we only reach the center of functional analysis when we consider how ritual and myth help man face those experiences in life when his ordinary defenses against the dangers of existence are threatened or found to be inadequate. Thomas O'Dea has succinctly summarized these dimensions as contingency (or uncertainty), powerlessness, and scarcity. Often we are uncertain about the course of events that affect our prosperity and good fortune. We are afflicted with the sense of helplessness as we find ourselves impotent to control events according to our own chosen goals. Or, again, nature does not provide with sufficient abundance for our needs.

Such situations lead to frustration and deprivation. Ritual and myth are used to deal with this aspect of human experience in a number of ways. Man may seek to enhance ordinary powers through magical spells. Perhaps he is encouraged to greater effort by rituals that sustain hope and keep confidence alive. Again, he may find in a sacred story consolation and the means to accept that which cannot be changed so that personality disintegration through anxiety and grief is prevented.

Too often this point is made by the modern observer in a curiously detached manner that seems to preclude his own involvement in a human and cosmic situation common to all. Tribal man faces the problem of the "limit-situation" not as the result of his stupidity, superstition, or technological lack. The relation between man and his environment has been such from the dawn of history to the present hour that "contingency, powerlessness, and scarcity" are not expressions of subjective fear only, but appropriate descriptions of the objective relationship of man to nature. Modern man has increased his power through technological efficiency. The fact still remains that he does not know when and if his nation will be destroyed in an atomic war or if national prosperity will continue. The individual man still does not know what accident or illness may suddenly strike him in the midst of an affluent society.

If we once recognize this aspect of our own contemporary situation, we can better appreciate the meaningfulness of the *depth problem* primitive man acknowledges, whether or not we decide to accept his particular solution. John Dewey makes the point with telling accuracy:

> *It is an old saying that the gods were born of fear. The saying is only too likely to strengthen a misconception bred by confirmed subjective habits. We first endow man in isolation with an instinct of fear and then we imagine him irrationally ejecting that fear into the environment, scattering broadcast as it were, the fruits of his own purely personal limitations, and thereby creating superstition. But fear, whether an instinct or an acquisition, is a function of the environment. Man fears because he exists in a fearful, an awful world. The world is precarious and perilous. It is as easily accessible and striking evidence of this fact that primitive experience is cited. The voice is that of early man; but the hand is that of nature, the nature in which we still live.*[20]

Furthermore, we must be careful not to state this situation in too narrowly instrumental a manner. The problem man faces is not simply one of finding a means to gain the power or method that can overcome or subvert the effects of the humanly frustrating aspects of nature, though this personal instrumental need is certainly important. More significant, however, is the problem, indeed the *crisis,* generated in man by the occurrence of tragic events which he cannot satisfactorily integrate into his system of beliefs and values.

This is the *problem of meaning* which existential philosophers argue still perplexes modern man. It is true that many modern thinkers rather insist that it is "the question of meaning" itself that is "meaningless." It is not necessary for us to engage here in this philosophical dispute, but it is important to see that whatever may be our decision about the logical viability of the problem according to present-day norms of intelligibility, descriptive accuracy forces us to recognize the problem as a real one in the tribal patterns we are examining. We would add that it also afflicts modern man as well, whether or not this discloses a logical confusion on his part.

Fundamentally, the problem is an existential one concerning the fate of the individual within the wider nexus of natural events. When disease or disaster strikes a person, he may be initiated into a confused and disintegrated state of personal being in which the question of "Why?" or even more directly "Why me?" is an inevitable response. What does such a question mean? The person may have a very clear notion of the causal chain of events that led to tragedy. This does not prevent him from experiencing shock, confusion, alienation.

Evidently the shock is generated by a sense of inner dislocation, a felt incongruity between man and outer world taking place on an emotional and valuational level rather than a strictly logical or common-sense one. When the events of nature and his own desires coalesce in a set of successful goal-directed actions, man feels a

---

20. John Dewey, *Experience and Nature,* New York, Dover, 1958, p. 42.

sense of harmonious relation between himself and his world. Failure and frustration generate an inner sense of disharmony. One still perceives the external structure of the natural pattern, but he no longer feels that he either understands or appreciates it. He is emotionally and axiologically alienated from his world and its underlying significance. The question "Why?" is the expression of his alienation.

We can see the structure of the problem in the classic study of Azande witchcraft by Evans-Pritchard; he points out that it is a serious error to deem the Azande, an African tribe, to be ignorant or oblivious to a nexus of ordinary or natural causation among events. For example, if a granary collapses and injures people who were sitting under it to avail themselves of its shade, the Azande clearly understand the common-sense series of causes that led to the catastrophe. Termites had undermined the supports, a fact the Azande know and acknowledge. The motives that led the people to be sitting there are also obvious and understandable. The fact still remains that the Azande feel the need to add a further explanation— witchcraft—to explain, not why such events occur in general, but why this happened at that particular time and place to those particular people. Evans-Pritchard insists that the witchcraft explanation is not an alternative to ordinary common-sense explanations, but a supplement needed to meet the existential factor of the event as it afflicts a specific individual. Thus, "Fire is hot, but it is not hot owing to witchcraft, for that is its nature. It is a universal quality of fire to burn, but it is not a universal quality of fire to burn *you*. This may never happen; or once in a lifetime, and then only if you have been bewitched." [21]

We need not here decide whether tribal patterns finally "answer" this question. Since, as we have noted, its basic components are emotional and axiological rather than intellectual, the question is answered well enough on one level through rituals and myths that enable the person to overcome his emotional alienation and reestablish some kind of behavioral harmony with his world. As Clifford Geertz observes:

> *As a religious problem, the problem of suffering is, paradoxically, not how to avoid suffering but how to suffer, how to make of physical pain, personal loss, worldly defeat, or the helpless contemplation of others' agony something bearable, supportable— something, as we say, sufferable. . . . As religion on one side anchors the power of our symbolic resources for formulating analytic ideas in an authoritative conception of the overall shape of reality, so on another side it anchors the power of our, also symbolic, resources for expressing emotions—moods, sentiments, passions, affections, feelings—in a similar conception of its pervasive tenor, its inherent tone and temper. For those able to embrace them, and for so long as they are able to embrace them,*

21. E. E. Evans-Pritchard, *Witchcraft, Oracles and Magic Among the Azande,* London, Oxford, 1940, p. 69.

*religious symbols provide a cosmic guarantee not only for their
ability to comprehend the world, but also, comprehending it, to
give a precision to their feeling, a definition to their emotions
which enables them, morosely or joyfully, grimly or cavalierly, to
endure it.*[22]

How do religious rites and myths accomplish this purpose? A full
explanation is beyond the scope of this introductory survey and has
probably not yet been formulated. Furthermore, we must leave open
the possibility that religion does not fully accomplish its purpose but
merely makes a valiant attempt to do so.

However, a provisional explanation that fits a great deal of the
material and is in harmony with the emphasis of many contemporary historians of religion might call attention to the way in which
rite and myth enable the sufferer to feel that he is participating in a
cosmic drama transcending his private existence and in which his
personal pain is seen as a significant part of this larger meaningful
whole.

It is not suffering that is the problem so much as meaningless
suffering. Man can endure pain but not chaos. Says Geertz, quoting
Salvador de Madariaga, the minimal definition of religion might be
"the relatively modest dogma that God is not mad." [23] Through ritual and myth, man is able to correlate the inexplicable and unac-
ceptable elements of his life from the threat of this final incoher-
ence. His pain may still be terrible and heart-rending. It is not finally
unendurable.

Lévi-Strauss offers a fascinating account of how ritual and myth
accomplish this feat in his summary of the song sung by a Cuna
shaman (a tribal holy man possessing unusual powers) over a
woman suffering from a difficult childbirth. According to the song,
the shaman sets out for the house of Muu who is a spirit responsible for the fetus. She is not a fundamentally evil power, but a force
gone awry who destroyed the bodily health by disturbing the powers
belonging to various parts of the body and destroying the natural
harmony of that body. The shaman goes on a hazardous journey, a
descent into the depths where Muu is and which reminds us of the
initiation patterns of separation, descent, return, which we have already noted. In this case, what is so fascinating is that the encounter with various mythical powers can be seen to clearly correspond
to various parts of the woman's body, so that her suffering and
physical problems are rendered in the song as a part of a larger
cosmic drama. She faces on the conscious level the details of her
suffering through the mythical language of the song. In doing so,
she does not escape the pain, but it is rendered more bearable
through its participation in struggle with Muu, who is both a mythic
power and the vagina and womb of the pregnant woman.

Lévi-Strauss points out that such practices do effect cures. As the

22. Clifford Geertz, "Religion as a Cultural System," in M. Banton, ed.,
Anthropological Approaches to the Study of Religion, New York, Praeger,
1966, p. 19.
23. Ibid., p. 13.

shaman conquers Muu and returns from her stronghold, the woman may have successful birth. What has happened?

The cure would consist, therefore, in making explicit a situation originally existing on the emotional level and in rendering acceptable to the mind pains which the body refuses to tolerate . . . the tutelary spirits and malevolent spirits, the supernatural monsters and magical animals, are all part of a coherent system on which the native conception of the universe is founded. The sick woman accepts these mythical beings, or, more accurately, she has never questioned their existence. What she does not accept are the incoherent and arbitrary pains, which are an alien element in her system but which the shaman, calling upon the myth, will re-integrate within a whole where everything is meaningful.[24]

Lévi-Strauss continues:

The shaman provides the sick woman with a language, by means of which unexpressed, and otherwise, inexpressible, psychic states can be immediately expressed. And it is the transition to this verbal expression—at the same time making it possible to undergo in an ordered and intelligible form a real experience that would otherwise be chaotic and inexpressible—which induces the release of the physiological process, that is, the reorganization, in a favorable direction, of the process to which the sick woman is subjected.[25]

Even when a ritual does not purport to specifically cure an ill, it may in a general way perform the kind of function Lévi-Strauss describes. It is significant that most myths contain accounts of struggle and loss; rituals contain elements of pain and sacrifice. Through participation in these forms, the participant prepares himself for the encounter with tragedy; he does not escape his ordeal nor does he pretend to; but the total devastation of the pain is mitigated by its incorporation in a larger cosmic pattern. The alienation from an intractable world is overcome. Suffering man still belongs.

In this light we may appreciate Susanne Langer's apt observation:

Myth . . . at least at its best is a recognition of natural conflicts, of human desire frustrated by non-human powers, hostile oppression, or contrary desires; it is a story of the birth, passion, and defeat by death which is man's common fate. Its ultimate end is not wishful distortion of the world, but serious envisagement of its fundamental truths; moral orientation, not escape.[26]

THE EXPRESSIVE
FUNCTION OF
RITUAL AND MYTH

The obvious facts of the social functionality of ritual and myth cannot be denied. Yet something seems to be missing from the account. Many sociologists and philosophers have opened up a fresh

24. Claude Lévi-Strauss, *Structural Anthropology*, Garden City, N.Y., Doubleday Anchor, 1967, pp. 192–193.
25. Ibid., p. 193.
26. Susanne Langer, *Philosophy in a New Key*, New York, Mentor Books, 1964, p. 153.

avenue of approach by stressing another aspect of ritual and myth that functional analysis tended to neglect. The problem is that a functional approach encourages us to look at all human behavior in a purely practical and manipulative way. Functionality tends to be identified with instrumentality, so that each activity is considered as a *means* by which we accomplish some other goal external to the action itself. Activity is thought of as goal-oriented, and each specific action is the instrument or tool by which we hope to achieve a given aim.

However, we may begin to wonder, are all activities instrumental in this sense? If so, do we never reach our goals? Are we always on the way, and never arriving? Are there no activities which are not means to ends, but rather ends in themselves?

Two dimensions of human activity in particular accentuate these questions: play and art. What is the functionality of play? In answering this question, the perplexing issues that have plagued us in the preceding discussion are brought into sharper focus. We might want to argue that a child's play has obvious biological and psychological value. It can exercise bodily muscles, relax tensions, provide welcome interludes between tiring periods of study or work. Perhaps it generates learning under the guise of pleasure. Many parents cognizant of these possibilities encourage their children to play, convinced of the basic "usefulness" of such behavior. Yet if the child himself entered into his play activity with those goals in mind, the event would cease to be play. The deliberate attempt to activate bodily functions is called exercise, not play. Deliberate relaxation is called rest. The development of skills, even when enjoyable, is called learning. The distinguishing character of play is that it is spontaneous, unmotivated, an activity pursued exuberantly for its own sake. We can either say it has no goal (when defined as an aim external to the action itself) or that its goal is inherent in the action itself. The purpose of the behavior is in the behavior. It is not the means to some other end, but an end in itself.

Similarly, art may serve all kinds of subsidiary purposes. It may be used for instruction, an aid in psychological integration, or diversion of the mind from some unpleasant truth. However, the artist who produces the work is not primarily concerned with these kinds of instrumental goals. He delights in making the art product as an aesthetic entity, an end in itself. So we make a house to protect ourselves from the elements; but the artistic decorations of that house do not serve the same kind of practical purpose. Yet they are valued, appreciated, and make living in the house a rich human experience, not a matter of brute necessity alone.

We are not necessarily insisting that this observation comprises a fully adequate aesthetic theory. It is sufficient for our purposes to observe that the cultural activities of man reveal aspects in which play and aesthetic expression are as important, sometimes more important, than strictly instrumental and practical considerations.

John Dewey makes this point:

Human experience in the large, its course and conspicuous features, has for one of its most striking features preoccupation with direct enjoyment, feasting and festivities, ornamentation, dance, song, dramatic pantomime, telling yarns and enacting stories. In comparison with intellectual and moral endeavor, this trait of experience has hardly received the attention from philosophers that it demands. Even philosophers who have conceived that pleasure is the sole motive of man and the attainment of happiness his whole aim, have given a curiously sober, drab account of the working of pleasure and the search for happiness. Consider the utilitarians, how they toiled, spun, and wove, but who never saw man arrayed in joy as the lilies of the field. Happiness was to them a matter of calculation and effort, guided by mathematical book-keeping. The history of man shows however that man takes his enjoyment neat, and at as short range as possible. . . . The body is decked before it is clothed. While homes are still hovels, temples and palaces are embellished. Luxuries prevail over necessities except when necessities can be festally celebrated. Men make a game of their fishing and hunting. . . . Useful labor is, whenever possible, transformed by ceremonial and ritual accompaniments, subordinated to art that yields immediate enjoyment.[27]

When Dewey says that the play element has not received the attention from philosophers that it deserves, there are notable exceptions like John Huizinga and Susanne Langer. John Huizinga has written a classic on the play element in culture called *Homo Ludens*. He defines play as

voluntary activity or occupation executed within fixed limits of time and place, according to rules freely accepted but absolutely binding, having its aim in itself and accompanied by a feeling of tension, joy and the consciousness that it is "different" from "ordinary life."[28]

This point of the "difference" generated by play is important. Huizinga argues that an intriguing similarity between play and religious ritual is to be found in the way that both set apart a sort of area—the "play-ground" or the "holy place"—where their respective actions are pursued. "Formally speaking, there is no distinction whatever between marking out a space for a sacred purpose and marking it out for purposes of sheer play. The turf, the tennis-court, the chess board and pavement-hopscotch cannot formally be distinguished from the temple or the magic circle."[29]

Another point of similarity between play and ritual lies in the "play-acting" quality exhibited in both. Play quickly assumes the form of drama (which we commonly call "a play") where the actors assume identities different from their everyday personalities and simulate actions different from those performed in their practical

27. Dewey, op. cit., pp. 78–79.
28. John Huizinga, *Homo Ludens*, Boston, Beacon Press, 1950, p. 28.
29. Ibid., p. 20.

life. The participants in a ritual also often assume a special garb—ceremonial robes, for example—and roles different from their ordinary selves. We have seen how the Tikopia chief, for example, claimed to be the god during the time of ritual. This claim can be explained in various ways. Here we want to stress that the chief's action is analogous to that of an actor who assumes a role for the duration of the play.

There is in both play and ritual the sense of generating or creating "another world" where the action, separated from everyday concerns, is integrated into a "make-believe," "imaginary," or "magic" realm. The performers of a ritual introduce us to "another world" different from that of everyday practical life. We have already witnessed many examples in the preceding discussion where ritual and myth assume the form of play. In the ceremony of the hot food, the solemnity of a feast with the high god is interwoven with a kind of game (who can eat his hot yam first). The solemnities finish with laughing and humorous exchanges. In the initiation of the New Guinea youths, we have seen how the youths are frightened by stories of the monsters. Finally they discover that the monsters are really their fathers. They do not respond with anger at the "deception," but enjoy their participation in the dramatic play.

Certain semantic difficulties beset the analysis of play and art. Shall we say such activities are "goal-less" or rather that the "goal" is inherent in the action itself? Even if a person performs an action for no purpose external to the action itself, do we not still want to say that he has a "purpose" or "reason" for performing it? The philosopher Immanuel Kant characterized aesthetic experience as "purposiveness without purpose." Some decisions as to basic usage of these words is required. Perhaps we can say that all behavior without exception has a "function." It does something and when we have adequately determined what is being done, we discern its functionality. We then can observe that many functions are "instrumental," i.e., they are means to an end external to the behavior itself. Other functions are "expressive," i.e., their performance has a self-justifying quality absent from purely instrumental activities. We may also observe that acts can be both instrumental and expressive at the same time.

Insight into the play element of culture is a key that will probably unlock many doors to a more profound understanding of religion. Nevertheless, the point must not be exaggerated. Play is intimately related to ritual, but probably not identical with it. For example, the solemnity of many rituals and the rigidity with which some of their sequential patterns are followed seem different from the spirit of spontaneous play. Furthermore, play complements but does not exclude the instrumental aspect of life. Religion seems to operate in both realms and it is the intricate way in which practical purposes and expressive celebration are intertwined that make it so difficult to interpret in a single formula.

In this connection the relation between magic and religion that is often discussed in anthropological literature is significant.

Although many of the ideas of James Frazer about archaic religions have been rejected by later scholars, his description of magic is still illuminating. According to Frazer, primitive magic is based on two principles. One is that homeopathic magic is based on the principle of similarity. In this view, a picture of an object can be used to affect the condition of the object that it resembles. For example, if you stick pins into a doll the person whom the doll resembles will be hurt. A second principle of magic that Frazer notes is the law of contagion, whereby magical influences are based on physical contiguity. Thus a sorcerer can injure another person if he can obtain a bit of his hair, a nail clipping, a shred of his clothes, even the dust he has trodden. In these instances it seems as if the separate identities of things have been lost. A thing like another seems to become in some sense the other. The part (a bit of hair) becomes the whole (the person). What is done to the part affects the whole.

According to Frazer, magic in its pure state is completely unrelated to religion defined as an orientation toward spirits, gods, or other beings transcending the natural order of the physical cosmos. The magician "supplicates no higher power: he sues the favour of no fickle and wayward being: he abases himself before no awful deity. Yet his power, great as he believes it to be, is by no means arbitrary and unlimited. He can wield it only as he strictly conforms to the rules of his art, or to what may be called the laws of nature as conceived by him." [30] Frazer argued that the magician had greater affinities to the scientist than to the religionist. Both magician and scientist assume the succession of events to be "perfectly regular and certain, being determined by immutable laws, the operation of which can be foreseen and calculated precisely; the elements of caprice, of chance, and of accident are banished from the course of nature." [31]

The only difference between the two is that the magician employs a "total misconception of the nature of the particular laws which govern that sequence," since similarity and contiguity are not the basis of real causality in nature.

Malinowski accepted this distinction in the main, but with some interesting qualifications. He adds to Frazer's analysis the point that magic is individualistic while religion is predominantly social. Thus Malinowski argues that religion is expressed in myths and rituals that have a social import and in which the whole tribe participates, while magic is usually an affair in which a private individual seeks out the sorcerer in order to accomplish some specific personal goal, like the death of an enemy, the realization of love from a desired man or woman, cure for disease, the achievement of prosperity or victory in war.

According to this distinction, it seems that magic aspires to attain an essentially manipulative relation with the forces of nature. It wants to control them for personal ends. Religion, on the other

30. James Frazer, *The Golden Bough,* Vol. I, abridged edition, New York, Macmillan, 1958, p. 56.
31. Ibid., p. 56.

hand, seeks to enter into a *communal* relation with spiritual beings (the gods) who are more than impersonal forces. Religion may seek help from the gods, but it can only beseech, never command. We might expand this distinction by use of the famous categories "I-it" and "I-thou" propounded by Martin Buber. Magic in its pure form establishes a manipulative, I-it relation with nature; religion aspires to an I-thou relationship of personal meeting in which man seeks to serve and adore his god as much as he seeks to be served by him. Or again, using the terminology developed in the second chapter, magic is essentially concerned with the instrumental dimension of life, while religion emphasizes the expressive. Thus Malinowski points out that magic uses its techniques as means to external ends, while religion usually develops a social ritual that is an end in itself. He portrays "magic as a practical art consisting of acts which are only means to a definite end expected to follow later on; religion as a body of self-contained acts being themselves the fulfillment of their purpose." [32]

Although this distinction is useful for certain purposes, it encourages a wide separation of human practices that cannot be meaningfully maintained. We seldom, if ever, find in a human society the instance of magic as oblivious to the realm of personal spirits and gods as Frazer described. The magical element is not as purely manipulative nor the religious as nonmanipulative as is here suggested. Also, religion can be individualistic, and some magical ceremonies have a communal and social form to their enactment. Thus Raymond Firth, for example, observed:

> The Arika Kafika, in praying for rain to fertilize the crops, did not pour water on the ground or make motions to imitate clouds. He spoke of rain and clouds by way of appeal, and where he symbolized them he did so in verbal imagery and not by crude signs. So also in other respects the Tikopia pagan priest was much more allusive, much more "poetic" in his rite and formula than is the public functionary presented to us by Frazer.[33]

The fact is that we rarely, if ever, find in human culture an example of "pure" manipulative magic devoid of communal elements, or a pure religion that stresses only the I-thou relation with no thought of personal needs and goals at all. On the contrary, we find the instrumental and the expressive, the manipulative and the communal, in dynamic interaction.

This point has led William Goode to suggest that magic and religion should be conceived as polar variables rather than exclusive alternatives. In this view magic and religion should be conceived as existing along a single continuum, magic representing one extreme limit of total manipulation and religion the other extreme limit of communal expressiveness. Most examples fall somewhere in between and represent a magico-religious complex in which both poles may be in equilibrium or one or the other may predominate.

32. Malinowski, op. cit., p. 88.
33. *Work*, pp. 17–18.

Thomas O'Dea has admirably summarized the relation between magic and religion:

Religion has been defined in terms of functional theory as the manipulation of non-empirical or supraempirical means for non-empirical or supraempirical ends; magic as the manipulation of non-empirical or supraempirical means for empirical ends. But the use of the term "manipulation" in the definition of religion is inaccurate and fails to describe adequately the religious attitude. Religion offers what is felt to be a way of entering into a relationship with the supraempirical aspects of reality, be they conceived as God, gods, or otherwise. Magic differs from religion in that it is manipulative in essence; yet magical manipulation too is conducted in an atmosphere of fear and respect, marvel and wonder, similar to that which characterizes the religious relationship.[34]

An analogy of religion with ordinary human social relationships is here helpful. When we engage in a meaningful relation with another person, what is our motive? Is it the purely manipulative one of "getting something" from him. We can describe the relation in these terms, because even altruistic impulses like love can be converted into the form of a "need for love" which is satisfied by a relation with the other.

However, such language distorts the full complexity of what is taking place. It would be too unrealistic to say that a friend can never be of "use" to us; but neither is it accurate to say that we do not value the friendship for its own sake; it is a fact that we want to give to as well as get from the relationship, so that practical and communal concerns are intimately intertwined. In the same manner, the religious relationship probably contains within it both magical and communal elements in varying degrees of interaction.

One problem in the use of this distinction is that it seems to assume that religion, by definition, is a benign phenomenon contrasted with dehumanizing magic. It would seem more useful as an objective categorical tool to refer to manipulative and communal poles both of which participate in the phenomenon we call religion. Religion can assume a manipulative form when the gods are cajoled, begged, tricked, or forced into serving some limited human end. It can also have the more expansive, altruistic dimensions we have noted. By the same token, magic has in it elements that are more noninstrumental and expressive than is often recognized. Thus Langer argues that

whatever purpose magical practice may serve, its direct motivation is the desire to symbolize great conceptions. It is the overt action in which a rich and savage imagination automatically ends. Its origin is probably not practical at all, but ritualistic; its central aim is to symbolize a Presence, to aid in the formulation

34. Thomas O'Dea, *The Sociology of Religion*, Englewood Cliffs, N.J., Prentice-Hall, 1966, p. 7.

of a religious universe. . . . Magic is never employed in a commonplace mood, like ordinary causal agency; this fact belies the widely accepted belief that the "method of magic" rests on a mistaken view of causality. After all, a savage who beats a tom-tom to drive off his brother's malaria would never make such a practical mistake as to shoot his arrow blunt end forward or bait his fishline with flowers. It is not ignorance of causal relations, but the supervention of an interest stronger than his practical interest, that holds him to magical rites. This stronger interest concerns the expressive value of such mystic acts.

Magic, then, is not a method, but a language; it is part and parcel of that greater phenomenon, ritual, *which is the language of religion. Ritual is a symbolic transformation of experiences that no other medium can adequately express. Because it springs from a primary human need, it is a spontaneous activity—that is to say, it arises without intention, without adaptation to a conscious purpose; its growth is undesigned, its pattern purely natural, however intricate it may be. It was never "imposed" on people; they acted thus quite of themselves, exactly as bees swarmed and birds built nests, squirrels hoarded food, and cats washed their faces. No one made up ritual, any more than anyone made up Hebrew or Sanskrit or Latin. The forms of expressive acts—speech and gesture, song and sacrifice—are the symbolic transformations which minds of certain species, at certain stages of their development and communion, naturally produce.*[35]

We conclude that a proper account of religious phenomena must include recognition of both instrumental and expressive elements. In the end, the distinction between them should not be made in a sharp and exclusive manner. Actually, instrumental symbols have an expressive element and expressive symbols are functional and even instrumental in some sense. The recognition of the expressive character of religious symbols will keep us from approaching them with a heavy, hyperserious frame of mind that misses their exuberant, creative, often playful character. Many religious acts and symbols are both means to an end and an end in themselves.

---

35. Langer, op. cit., p. 52.

RELIGION AS SYMBOLIC EXPRESSION: THE INTERPRETATION OF MYTH

THE HERMENEUTICAL
APPROACH TO RELIGION

In the preceding chapter we considered how ritual actions perform various functions for human beings in their personal and social lives. In the course of this examination we have seen how doing and meaning are inextricably connected. Ritual acts are themselves highly symbolic. Furthermore, myths, emblems, and other symbolic devices are often used in conjunction with ritual to convey complex meanings. In this chapter we want to look at religious phenomena primarily as modes of symbolic expression.

At the present time great interest exists among scholars from a variety of fields in the phenomenon of human symbolism. Psychologists study the symbols man forms in his dreams. Archeologists look for the significance of human artifacts from ancient civilizations. Mathematicians and logicians have made great advances in understanding how systems of very abstract signs operate. Linguists, philologists, and semanticists have investigated the function of meaning in human language. Some contemporary philosophies have turned to a consideration of problems generated by the "uses" of language. Susanne Langer therefore argues in *Philosophy in a New Key* that the emphasis on symbolization is the "key" to contemporary thought taken as a whole. The focus of attention has turned from what a man says to the symbolic modes by which he says it, though the two aspects are, of course, intricately related.

It is this entire approach that we here call the hermeneutical

perspective. We might with equal appropriateness call it the semiological approach, but this term has come to be associated with one
specific school within the entire spectrum of studies of symbolism.
"Hermeneutics" is also used in a narrower sense to refer to the
techniques by which scholars interpret the meanings of written documents. For example, in the study of Judaism and Christianity the
interpretation of the biblical writings is called hermeneutics. However, for want of a better word we use the term here in a broader
sense to include all attempts to interpret the meanings of any kind
of symbol whatsoever. As Mircea Eliade puts it:

> *By means of a competent hermeneutics, history of religions
> ceases to be a museum of fossils, ruins, and obsolete mirabilia
> and becomes what it should have been from the beginning for
> any investigator: a series of "messages" waiting to be deciphered
> and understood.*[1]

The approach to the study of man through the act of symbolization thus has important implications for the study of religion. Let us
look at some of the presuppositions of this approach.

THE
SYMBOL-MAKING
ANIMAL

Man has been defined in different ways. For example, he has been
called the rational animal, the religious animal, the tool-making
animal. According to the emphasis of contemporary thought, he
is frequently defined as the symbol-making animal. Symbols should
be distinguished from signals or "triggers." Animals, for example,
can respond to various sounds or smells that trigger certain actions.
Thus an animal hunting another animal finds that the smell of that
animal is a "trigger" that directs his movements toward the one
hunted.

Human beings also respond to signals. But in addition, human
beings are able to distinguish between the sign and the thing signified by it and to perceive the symbolic relation between them. For
example, language is an obvious illustration of the human symbolic
capacity. Combinations of sounds are used as symbolic counters to
mean various aspects of human experience. Yet the sounds have no
intrinsic connection with what they mean; the relation between the
two is a symbolic one established by man's capacity to distinguish
between sign and the thing signified.

Man uses many other kinds of phenomena besides sounds as
symbolic devices. For example, facial expressions are symbolic, as
the phrase implies. A smile means pleasure or approval; a frown indicates displeasure or disapproval. A hunter marks a tree or puts a
twig on the ground pointing a certain way; a man who later reaches
this place interprets the symbolic vehicles as meaning that the
hunter has gone ahead in a given direction. A man may paint his
body or put on certain kinds of clothing which indicate the status or
role that he has assumed in a given society.

1. Mircea Eliade, *The Quest*, Chicago, The University of Chicago Press,
1969, preface.

Some common religious symbols. Top to bottom: chi-rho; swastika; yin-yang; mandala.

Religion provides a striking and extremely widespread example of man's symbolic activity. Religions throughout the world have made use of various phenomena of nature and human culture to serve as symbolic devices through which complex meanings are conveyed. For example:

1. *Sounds.* Certain exclamations and sacred cries are used in tribal religious rites. In the Upanishads of Hinduism we learn of a sacred sound or word, *om.*

2. *Myths expressed in language.* As we have seen, sacred stories are often told that convey complex meanings.

3. *Beliefs expressed in language.* Many religions contain a set of statements about man, the world, and the gods that are orally transmitted or set down in writing.

4. *Rituals.* As we saw in the last chapter, ceremonial actions are used to convey religious meanings.

5. *Colors.* Colors or combinations of colors can be used as symbols. Green has been taken to mean fertility, red sacrifice, and so forth.

6. *Emblems.* Distinctive forms like a cross, a swastika, the yin-yang circle, are used to convey complex meanings.

7. *Natural objects.* Stones, trees, rivers, mountains, have been used in various religions as symbols with sacred significance.

8. *Buildings.* Religious edifices often have symbolic intentions as well as functional utility. For example, some Christian churches deliberately take the form of a cross. Islamic mosques face Mecca, and so forth.

This brief list is in no sense exhaustive of the symbolic possibilities in religion. There is no phenomenon of nature or human thought that cannot be used as a religious sign.

Many helpful studies of religious symbols have been made by modern scholars. One difficulty for the beginning student is caused by the fact that there is no common agreement in the voluminous literature on how words like "sign" and "symbol" are to be used. The student must learn how such terms are defined by a given writer and recognize the fact that another writer may define them differently.

Often the terms "sign" and "symbol" are used as synonyms to refer to the entire range of devices that can be used to convey meanings. Sometimes a distinction is made between a sign which has one direct meaning and a symbol which is more complex and conveys many meanings through a single vehicle. For example, Susanne Langer describes presentational symbols that combine a number of meanings into a single comprehensive and unitary form. Thus an animal might respond to a drop of splashing water as the natural signal of a river nearby. A human being may, in addition, use the word "water" as a linguistic sign of that same river. Or again, he may paint a picture of that river which now functions as a presentational symbol. What does the symbol mean? The significations are complex and multiform. Perhaps it still refers to the physical river, but in addition conveys memories of the refreshing quality of water in general and its value for human life. Perhaps the painting is put in a religious temple and is interpreted in connection with a need for the spiritual water of eternal life or the need of ritual cleansing from moral defilement. The notion of the physical river is now subordinated to the idea of moral cleansing and that which quenches a "spiritual" thirst. Many religions use the symbol of water in these complex ways.

Paul Tillich makes a distinction between sign and symbol that is similar but not identical with that of Langer. To Tillich the former points to a single object in an external and largely instrumental manner. A symbol, as Tillich sees it, not only points to its referent, but in some sense, seems to the user of the symbol to participate in it. For example, the phrase "United States" is a "sign" referring to a certain country. The American flag is a "symbol" that somehow shares in the reality that it represents. Consequently, respect shown the flag is respect for the country itself. Symbol and symbolized are integrally connected.

It is obvious that the religions of the world display many such symbols like the Buddhist lotus flower, the yin-yang symbol of the Chinese, the Jewish star of David, the Christian cross. An adequate interpretation of any religion must include an engagement with its most fundamental symbols. Emblems and icons, architectural shapes, colors, natural objects like stones or mountains, can assume such a symbolic significance according to the religious context in which they are placed.

An awareness of the symbolic texture of religion can help us avoid interpretations of religious forms that are simplistic or reductionist. Too often we treat a religious expression as if it conveyed one single meaning that can easily be understood on some literal level of significance restricted to the external apprehension of the physical world.

A typical totempole of the Northwest Coast Indians. (Courtesy of the American Museum of Natural History.)

However, we have already seen evidence that rituals and myths have the capacity for symbolic condensation whereby a number of interacting meanings are conveyed simultaneously. It is this insight that helps us to see that the various interpretations of ritual we have so far considered are complementary meanings rather than exclusive alternatives. The Tikopia rite, for example, can refer to social relations, personal problems, depth meanings concerning limit questions, and the realm of the gods simultaneously through their amazing symbolic capacity to compress the manifold dimensions of existence into unifying symbolic forms.

Recently a number of scholars have sought to develop a new science called semiology which is distinct from though related to linguistics. Linguistics is the study of the structures of language. Important work has been done in this field by such figures as R. Jakobson, M. Halle, N. Chomsky, among others. Ferdinand de Saussure was a pioneer in the study of linguistics who considered the possibility of a more comprehensive study of symbolism that would include other systems of meaning beside language. Thus one of his disciples, Roland Barthes, defines semiology as the study of

THE SEMIOLOGICAL APPROACH TO RELIGION

any system of signs, whatever their substance and limits; images, gestures, musical sounds, objects, and the complex associations of all these, which form the content of ritual, convention, or public entertainment: these constitute, if not languages, *at least systems of signification.*[2]

This last phrase is important. We are all aware that a language is not a mere collection of sounds. To be a language, the sounds must be patterned into words according to the laws of phonetics. Then the words must be arranged according to the rules of syntax. For example, in Indo-European languages certain words called nouns are connected with other words called verbs according to very specific rules of how they can be related. It is clear that a language is a system of sounds arranged in a certain way. The student of a language does not merely study each individual sound or word made up of a combination of sounds. He also studies the structure or system whereby the words are arranged into meaningful patterns.

Now it is the thesis of the semiologists that other symbolic entities besides sounds are also arranged together according to definite structural laws. By analogy we could call them "languages" composed of their own kinds of symbolic counters. In the interest of clarity, Barthes suggests that they should rather be called "systems of signification" which are like languages in that they follow structural laws similar to those that operate in languages.

To make clear how sets of symbolic devices can exhibit structures similar to a language, let us look at some simple examples. Consider a system of traffic lights as it operates in many Western societies. Green means go, red means stop, yellow means caution. Here a relation among three colors is used to signify a relation among three possible actions. Red is to green is to yellow as stopping is to moving is to a cautionary pause between stopping and going. It is important here to see that the structure is more important than the surface qualities of the symbols used. Any other three colors, or these three colors applied differently, would do as well. What is important is that the person perceive the structural relation among the three colors and its congruence with a structural relation among three actions that are possible for him to perform.

Another more complicated example that might be used is the way that foods are structured in a given society. In a restaurant a menu provides a pattern in which the various items of food are organized. The hors d'oeuvres are distinguished from the main courses and these are distinguished from the desserts. Furthermore, the way foods are arranged has many symbolic functions. Thus, as a person chooses a certain wine to go with a certain kind of meat or fish, he often thereby indicates the class in society that he occupies. In preliterate societies, foods are also arranged according to how they are cooked, boiled, roasted, etc., and various meanings are attached to these arrangements.

Similarly clothes can be shown to form a system of signification.

2. Roland Barthes, *Elements of Semiology*, London, Cape, 1967, p. 9.

The world of fashion indicates the way individual items—the hat which goes with certain dresses and shoes only—are arranged into a pattern with definite meaning. By one's system of clothes arrangement he shows whether he is a businessman, a student, an industrious person, a "swinger," and so forth. In preliterate societies the arrangement of clothing and color has an even more obvious function of symbolizing various roles played in the society in question.

These then are examples of how individual items from the world of nature or human culture can be combined into a "system of signification." Semiological theory offers a very technical account of how this is done. To understand the theory in detail, the student will have to master important distinctions between language and speech, signified and signifier, syntagm and system, denotation and connotation. Very precise definitions are given to terms like sign, symbol, system, structure, and so on. We have attempted here simply to impart to the student a very general idea of what is meant by "system of signification" and "structure." The interested student is referred to works cited in the bibliography that can help him proceed further with this kind of analysis.

Claude Lévi-Strauss is an influential anthropologist in France who has been strongly influenced by semiological theory. He has sought to apply semiological principles to the study of man in preliterate societies. His methods and those of others moving in the same direction are often called "structuralism." Since this movement is presently very influential and has important implications for the study of religious phenomena, it will be useful here to consider further some aspects of its approach to religious symbolism. Let us look at one specific kind of religious symbol—myth—and see how a structuralist examines it.

Lévi-Strauss has devoted a great deal of attention to the study of myths and many examples of his approach are to be found in his monumental three volume work, *Mythologiques*. However, for the beginning student, the clearest and most accessible example of how he applies structural principles to the study of myth can be found in his essay "The Story of Asdiwal." [3]

THE STORY OF ASDIWAL

The story of Asdiwal is to be found in the culture of the Tsimshian Indians who live in British Columbia, immediately south of Alaska, in a region which embraces the basins of the Nass and Skeena rivers and is on the northwest Pacific coast. The anthropologist Franz Boaz has recorded several versions of the story which are examined by Lévi-Strauss. The following is a highly condensed summary of the story:

Two women, a mother and daughter, lived in the Skeena valley. The mother lived down-river in the west with her husband and the daughter lived up-river in the east with hers. Both husbands died

3. Claude Lévi-Strauss, "The Story of Asdiwal," in G. Leach, ed., *The Structural Study of Myth and Totemism*, London, Tavistock Publications, 1967, pp. 1–48.

of hunger. Winter came and a famine occurred. Both women si-multaneously desired to be reunited. They traveled on the frozen bed of the Skeena River, one traveling eastward and the other westward. They met half-way and pitched camp. During the night a stranger named Hatsenas (meaning bird of good omen) visited them and took the daughter as his wife. From their union was born Asdiwal. The father gave him various magic objects: a bow and arrow which never missed, a quiver, a lance, a basket, snow-shoes, a bark raincoat, and a hat which rendered the wearer in-visible. With these tools, Asdiwal provided an inexhaustible sup-ply of food for the group.

Hatsenas disappeared and the elder of the two women died. Asdiwal and his mother then traveled westward to the mother's native village. One day Asdiwal saw a white she-bear and fol-lowed her as she climbed a vertical ladder into the sky. At the top was a heavenly prairie covered with grass and flowers. The bear revealed herself as a beautiful woman named Evening Star who was the daughter of the Sun. Asdiwal went through a series of tests arranged by the Sun after which he was allowed to marry Evening Star.

Asdiwal began to pine for his mother. He and his wife were al-lowed to return to earth with food for the mother and her kins-men who were starving. Asdiwal then had relations with a woman of the village. Evening Star, offended, returned to her home on high. Asdiwal followed but half-way up was struck dead by a look from his wife. He was then brought back to life by his celes-tial father-in-law and for a time lived with his wife on high.

Again he pined for earth. His wife accompanied him to earth and then bade him a final farewell. Asdiwal then discovered that his mother had died. He traveled downstream to another village where he married the daughter of a local chief. His relations with the four brothers of his wife were marked by rivalry and strife. Asdiwal showed his superiority to the brothers in hunting bears in the mountains. Humiliated and enraged, the brothers took their sister and abandoned Asdiwal.

Asdiwal met another group of four brothers and again married their sister. Their union gave birth to a son. Again there was ri-valry. This time Asdiwal demonstrated his superiority in hunting sea lions. In the process this time Asdiwal killed the hostile broth-ers with the help of his wife.

Again Asdiwal felt a desire to visit the scenes of his childhood. He left his wife and returned to the Skeena valley where he was joined by his son to whom he gave his magic bow and arrows.

When winter came Asdiwal went off to the mountains to hunt, but forgot his snowshoes. Without them, he could go neither up or down. He was turned to stone and can still be seen in that form at the peak of the great mountain.[4]

How is this myth to be interpreted? In order to see more clearly what is distinctive about a structural answer to this question, let us first consider other useful ways the story can be approached.

4. This account is my condensation of ibid., pp. 4–7.

A Tshimshian tribesman in full regalia. (*Courtesy of the American Museum of Natural History.*)

First of all, a Freudian might be interested in the recognition of a common oedipal situation expressed in the myth. According to Freud, all males go through a childhood process whereby they are strongly attracted toward their mother and view their father as a rival. Later they learn to identify themselves with their father and to free themselves from their early emotional attachment to the mother. The Greek myth of Oedipus reveals the situation in which this process of identification with the father is not successfully completed. Through a set of tragic mistakes, Oedipus killed his father and married his mother. The result was that he was blinded, i.e., prevented from maturing into a confident adult.

A follower of Freud would probably see in the story of Asdiwal traces of this problem. Asdiwal leaves his mother and goes to live with a father figure, the Sun, who lives in a world on high. However, atavistic longings to return to the mother overwhelm him and lead to a series of difficulties.

A follower of Jung might accept this interpretation but add other features as well. Jung believed that many symbols appearing in myths and dreams are archetypal forms that are part of the collective unconsciousness of mankind. According to Jung, these archetypal forms represent common patterns of events and psychological forces in which all human beings are involved. Thus a follower of Jung would probably see Asdiwal as the archetypal hero who overcomes various obstacles in order to achieve self-integration and bring gifts of healing and order to human society. When Asdiwal hunts the bear, later transformed into a beautiful woman, we have echoes of archetypal myths in which the hero subdues various monsters as a prelude to his assumption of power and authority. Asdiwal's meeting with the Sun is another archetypal situation as is his later death and resurrection.

Mircea Eliade, on the other hand, sees myths as sacred exemplary tales told in preliterate societies and archaic civilizations to express the conviction of a fundamental relationship between the profane world of human life and the sacred world of the primordial gods. Thus,

> in such societies the myth is thought to express the absolute truth, because it narrates a sacred history; that is, a transhuman revelation which took place at the dawn of the Great Time, in the holy time of the beginnings (in illo tempore). Being real and sacred, the myth becomes exemplary, and consequently repeatable, for it serves as a model, and by the same token as a justification, for all human actions. In other words, a myth is a true history of what came to pass at the beginning of Time, and one which provides the pattern for human behaviour. In imitating the exemplary acts of a god or of a mythic hero, or simply by recounting their adventures, the man of an archaic society detaches himself from profane time and magically re-enters the Great Time, the sacred time.[5]

Now an interpretation of the story of Asdiwal following this approach would no doubt stress the way that a sacred world on high is connected with the world of man and nature by a ladder. In many myths throughout the world one can find references to a ladder, rope, or pole connecting heaven and earth. The story of Asdiwal can be interpreted as one example of stories of how a primal hero brings the gifts of culture to man after he has made contact with the sacred world of the mythic gods.

Now Lévi-Strauss has provided us with a structural analysis of this story. The first point to see is that his approach does not differ from the others on matters of detail about what this figure or the other means (e.g., the ladder, the bear, the sun, the hero). Lévi-Strauss rather argues that the first step is to perceive how the various parts or elements of the myth are related together. In other words, he is less interested in the meanings of the specific elements of the myth than he is in the pattern of relationships by which they

5. Mircea Eliade, *Myths, Dreams and Mysteries*, New York, Collins, 1968, p. 23.

are bound together. To put it another way, he is less interested in the individual signs than he is in the "system of signification" by which they are put together into a meaningful whole.

In this connection, Lévi-Strauss offers another interesting analogy. In French society a *bricoleur* is a kind of handyman who collects miscellaneous objects like pieces of discarded machinery which he then uses in unconventional ways. He may, for example, improvise a new tool out of discarded items to perform a specific task like cleaning a chimney. Lévi-Strauss calls the myth-maker a kind of *bricoleur* who takes various images and symbols from his culture and combines them in unexpected ways to convey his meanings. Lévi-Strauss's point is that we should not look at the individual parts of the myth in isolation. It is the way they are combined together into a "system of signification" that is important.

For example, consider again our traffic light systems. We might wonder why red is chosen to mean stop and green to mean go. Is there some psychological reason why red is taken for the negative and green for the positive? Is red associated with blood and death; is green associated with fertility of plant life? Perhaps so. But a structuralist is more interested in the arrangement or structure of the colors in this particular system. Any other three colors would do as well. In fact, colors are not necessary. We might use dots. One dot is to two dots is to three dots as stop is to go is to caution. It is the structural arrangement of the parts, not the parts themselves, that is important. Similarly, in a given myth, it is more important to perceive the arrangement among the parts than to look at the meaning of each part in isolation from the others.

To see how this is done in practice, let us consider how Lévi-Strauss approaches the story of Asdiwal. He distinguishes a number of schema implicit in the story. First is a geographical schema. The figures in the story move in various directions throughout the story which may be schematized as follows:

```
                    NORTH
        EAST· · · · · · >WEST· · · · · · >EAST
                    SOUTH
```

Second there is a cosmological schema:

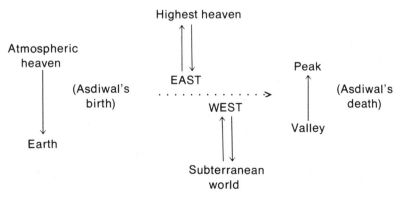

These schema in turn reflect a very general pattern of binary oppositions and integrations. For example:

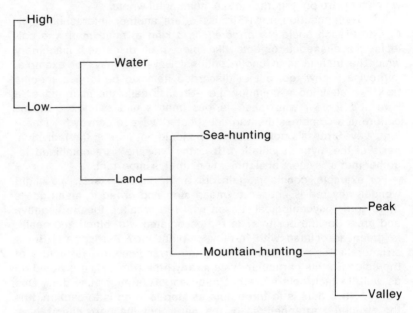

According to Lévi-Strauss these schema and others interact with one another to form a complex whole. Here a musical analogy is helpful. A musical score contains a set of relationships between sounds on a horizontal level that is called the melody. It also contains a set of vertical relations among notes that is called the harmony. Some forms of music involve counterpoint in which one melody moves horizontally at the same time that it interacts vertically with another melody as well. In the same way, according to Lévi-Strauss, a myth is like a musical score in that vertical and horizontal structures interact and convey a number of complex meanings simultaneously.

To make this clear, let us look at another schema Lévi-Strauss discovers in the story of Asdiwal. This is a sociological schema:

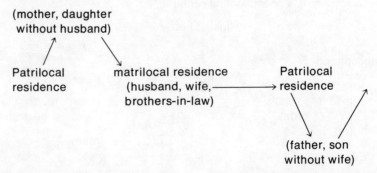

What does this schema mean? In their actual existence, the Tsimshian Indians have a system of social order based on matrilineal filiation and patrilocal residence. This means that when a man and woman marry, they go to live in the husband's village. Nevertheless, the children are considered to belong to the mother's clan and not the father's. Now such a system might be expected to generate various kinds of practical tensions among the generations, since the children are living among one group of people in the father's village but continue to have a cultural identification with the mother's clan.

In the story of Asdiwal this tension is explored through the structural arrangement of the sociological schema. In the beginning the deaths of their husbands lead the women to reject their patrilocal residence and return to a matrilocal one. Hatsenas marries Asdiwal's mother and lives with her (matrilocal residence). Asdiwal marries Evening Star and lives with her father (matrilocal residence). Asdiwal's second and third marriages are also matrilocal ones in which he lives with his wives' brothers. However, the situation is rife with tension. Finally, Lévi-Strauss points out,

> patrilocality triumphs when Asdiwal abandons his wife (whereas, in the previous marriages, it had been his wife who had abandoned him) and returns to the Skeena where he was born, and where his son comes alone to join him. Thus having begun with the story of the reunion of a mother and her daughter, freed from their affines or paternal kin, the myth ends with the story of the reunion of a father and his son, freed from their affines or maternal kin.[6]

According to Lévi-Strauss, the story of Asdiwal does not provide a solution to the sociological tensions experienced by the Tsimshian Indians. It rather explores and expresses the tension through the structural arrangement we have considered. In the end the immobility of Asdiwal (turned into stone) indicates that a completely satisfactory solution to the tension between patrilocal and matrilineal practices has not been found.

Other tensions are also exhibited in the structure of the story. For example, the alternatives between plenty and famine reflect the way the Tsimshians would collect a store of smoked fish and dried meat during the summer when they fished and hunted bears and goats in the mountains. At the end of winter their store of food was often exhausted and they endured periods of severe famine until they were able to fish again in the spring. Also, the Tsimshians moved according to the seasons between their winter villages and their summer fishing places. These structures are reflected in the geographical movements of Asdiwal in the story.

Lévi-Strauss goes into many details of these various schema that we cannot reproduce here. Enough has been presented to show how a structural analysis proceeds. To return to our musical analogy, we have seen how Lévi-Strauss argues that a myth proceeds through an intersection of patterns, like harmony and melody, or two melodies in counterpoint, to indicate the complexities of Tsimshian existence.

6. Lévi-Strauss, op. cit., pp. 12–13.

It is important to see that Lévi-Strauss's structural analysis is not an alternative to the other approaches to myth that we have indicated. Myths are about psychological, sociological, cosmological, and transcendent themes. All these are clearly in the story of Asdiwal. The structural analysis simply shows that these materials are organized into schemata or structures that help to elucidate the meaning. Although the structuralist emphasizes the structure as against the parts of which the structure is composed, he is still interested in what the structure means. As Lévi-Strauss put it in his discussion of the story of Asdiwal: "Having separated out the codes, we have analysed the structure of the message. It now remains to decipher the meaning." We have already considered examples of how this is done.

THE PROBLEM OF THE "PRELOGICAL" MIND

The structural approach that we have outlined here has important light to shed on the nature of religious symbolization taken as a whole. Often the forms of expression used in preliterate myths appear to the modern observer unfamiliar with them as devoid of precise meaning and intellectual order. For example, at first glance the story of Asdiwal seems to be a chaotic succession of events that have no central point. Indeed, our brief summary of the story left out a host of details that contribute even more to the general impression that it is a formless story that is the product more of a kind of mindless reverie than of thought.

Furthermore, mythic expressions seem to be oblivious to important distinctions. In the preceding chapter we saw how the Arika chief declared that he is the god Arika Kafika even while he is a human being. Again the Cuna shaman went on a journey both to the realm of the gods and into the sick woman's body at one and the same time.

Such usages are more than accidental in primitive cultures. They occur in all kinds of situations and seem to deny basic differentiations between separate things and between levels of reality. This aspect of primitive expressions has caused some scholars to speculate on the possibility that the "primitive mind" may operate according to principles or categories of thought that are in some ways different from those of civilized man. Thus Lucien Levy-Bruhl characterized native thought as determined by what he called the law of participation. According to this way of thinking,

> objects, beings, phenomena can be, though in a way incomprehensible to us, both themselves and something other than themselves. In a fashion no less incomprehensible, they give forth and they receive mystic powers, virtues, qualities, influences, which make themselves felt outside, without ceasing to remain where they are.[7]

7. Lucien Levy-Bruhl, *How Natives Think*, New York, Washington Square Press, 1966, p. 61.

In many books Levy-Bruhl called this kind of thinking "prelogical," by which he meant a kind of thought that

does not bind itself down, as our thought does, to avoiding contradiction. It obeys the law of participation first and foremost. Thus oriented, it does not expressly delight in what is contradictory (which would make it merely absurd in our eyes), but neither does it take pains to avoid it. It is often wholly indifferent to it, and that makes it so hard to follow.[8]

The philosopher Ernst Cassirer was also influenced by this notion. Cassirer argued that preliterate man not only composed specific myths, but organized his world according to a mythic form of organization. According to the rules of this mythic form of thought, the sense of the separate identity of different entities is not present. On the contrary, in mythic thought one object can easily be transformed into another, and to put the matter more strongly yet, can be both itself and the other at the same time. Thus in the story of Asdiwal we encounter a bear who is also a beautiful woman. No surprise that this transformation takes place because, Cassirer would argue, according to the laws of mythic thought such transformations are quite natural. Similarly, the woman's father seems to be both the physical sun seen in the sky *and* some kind of primordial father figure living in the heavenly prairie.

Levy-Bruhl later expressed doubts about his own notion of a "prelogical" mentality and most contemporary anthropologists have rejected it. The problem with this notion is that it implies a radical difference between the cognitive processes of primitive and civilized man. Western man adheres to a tradition of logic exemplified by Aristotle's presentation. In his works are found the three traditional canons of logic: the law of identity ($A = A$), the law of the excluded middle (A is either A or not A—there is no other possibility), and the law of noncontradiction (A cannot be both A and not A at the same time and in the same sense). Are we to believe that primitive man is oblivious to such distinctions? Data provided by anthropologists show us that, in fact, primitive peoples are capable of careful distinctions and differentiations.

We might well wonder if a being could survive if unable to make and hold on to distinctions between, for example, hot and cold, friend and enemy, food and poison. Here survival seems to depend on the ability to perceive such differences. Furthermore, there is no marked difference in the physiology, the nervous system, the brain structure, of primitives and civilized peoples. It is hardly likely, then, that primitives perceive their world at the level of the physical senses in a markedly different way than do civilized persons.

Specific anthropological studies support these suppositions. Primitive man may not make the same distinctions as do members of a civilization. Nevertheless, he has a sharp eye for detail and distinguishes carefully between phenomena according to his own pur-

8. Ibid., p. 63.

poses and interests. For example, the Hanunóo of the Philippines classify all forms of the local avifauna into seventy-five categories; they distinguish about a dozen kinds of snakes, sixty-odd types of fish, more than a dozen types of fresh and salt water crustaceans; every child of the Ryukyu archipelago can look at a tiny wood fragment and, by considering its bark, smell, hardness, make an identification according to his categories of classification. Such examples can be multiplied almost ad infinitum.

Furthermore, many primitive cultures, when examined carefully, can be shown to exhibit more subtlety and sophistication in expression than may at first be acknowledged. For example, we are aware of distinctions between literal assertions (the king is the ruler of the land; metonyms (the land is subject to the crown); similes (the king is like a lion); metaphors (the king is a lion). Primitive language often reveals similar forms which are not taken by the user with a greater degree of literalness than we do ourselves.

Thus, Evans-Pritchard insists that among native societies like the Nuer, the verb "to be" should not be interpreted as always meaning identity, any more than it is with us. For example, the Nuer say that in certain circumstances a cucumber is an ox and that it can therefore be substituted for an ox in a ritual sacrifice (see the following chapter). Nevertheless, the Nuer have not lost sight of the difference between an ox and a cucumber. Thus they never make the relation a symmetrical one, i.e., they never say that an ox is a cucumber. What is meant is that in certain circumstances (for example, where an ox is not available, probably because of the penury of the officiant) a cucumber may be treated *like* an ox.

Levy-Bruhl's notion of a "prelogical" mind is wrong in so far as it implies that preliterate men express themselves without regard to principles of structure and order. Nevertheless, it is also important to recognize that the structures and relations of preliterate societies involve metaphors and metonyms that are "poetic" rather than "scientific" without violating the laws of formal logic. As John Beattie puts it:

> Even though he overstated his case, Levy-Bruhl was right in emphasizing the poetical, analogical character of much "primitive" thinking. The predominantly scientific orientation of modern thought has much obscured the fact that peoples who are less concerned than Western Europeans are with scientific experimentation and logical method think about the world they live in in terms which are often symbolic and "literary" rather than scientific. This is no less true of European peasant cultures than it is of remote African or Oceanic tribes. We do the grossest injustice to the subtle allusive and evocative power of language if we require all meaningful verbal expression to conform to the rules of syllogism and inductive inference. Coherent thinking can be symbolic as well as scientific, and if we are sensible we do not subject the language of poetry to the same kind of examination that we apply to a scientific hypothesis.[9]

9. John Beattie, *Other Cultures*, New York, Free Press, 1964, pp. 68–69.

Furthermore, many preliterate rituals and myths express a sense of relationship between man and the world that is "participational" rather than "manipulative." For example, the sharp separation between animate beings and inanimate objects, common among people influenced by modern science, is profoundly minimized in primitive cultures. The attitude of primitive man in this connection is difficult to describe and further investigation is needed. It seems clear that primitive man behaves toward many objects we call inanimate—stones, for example—as though they were alive; the realm of natural objects as a whole seems to be animated and energetic.

However, the stance of primitive man should not be oversimplified in this respect. It is not the case that every object that he encounters is endowed with a personal soul exactly like his own. A. Irving Hallowell, for example, suggests that the Ojibwa (an American Indian tribe) exhibit a thought pattern in which "personhood" is a "cultural constituted cognitive set" that can include stones. "Whereas we should never expect a stone to manifest animate properties of any kind under any circumstances, the Ojibwa recognize, a priori, potentialities for animation in certain classes of objects under certain circumstances." [10] Thus, when Hallowell asked an old man whether all stones are alive, he answered, "No! But some are." He told of the experience of his father who during a sacred ceremony had seen a big round stone follow him around as he moved.

According to Hallowell, the Ojibwa thus recognize the possibility of personal dynamic properties in what people from a scientific culture would call inanimate objects. Nevertheless, such beliefs are *not* evidence of an illogical disordered "mind." On the contrary, as Hallowell argues, the belief can be shown to be part of a specific structural "cognitive set."

Such attitudes lead to a strong sense of communal relation between man and nature in preliterate societies. Dorothy Lee observes:

> *All economic activities, such as hunting, gathering fuel, cultivating the land, storing food, assume a relatedness to the encompassing universe, and, with many cultures, this is a religious relationship. In such cultures, men recognize a certain spiritual worth and dignity in the universe. They do not set out to control, or master, or exploit. Their ceremonials are periods of intensified communion, even social affairs, in a broad sense, if the term may be extended to include the forces of the universe. They are not placating or bribing or even thanking; they are rather in a formal period of concentrated enjoyable association.* [11]

10. A. Irving Hallowell, "Ojibwa Ontology, Behavior, and World View," in S. Diamond, ed., *Culture in History,* New York, Columbia, 1960, pp. 24–25.

11. Dorothy Lee, "Anthropology," in Hoxie N. Fairchild, et al., *Religious Perspectives in College Teaching,* New York, Ronald Press, 1952, pp. 340–341.

An old Wintu woman told Lee:

> *The white people never cared for the land or deer or bear. When we Indians kill meat, we eat it all up. . . . We shake down acorns and pinenuts. We don't cut down trees. We only use dead wood. But the white people plow up the ground, pull up the trees, kill everything. The tree says, "Don't, I am sore. Don't hurt me." But they chop it down and cut it up. The spirit of the land hates them. . . . How can the spirit of the land like the white man? Everywhere the white man has touched it, it is sore.*[12]

It is important here to see that there is no conflict between a recognition of such participational attitudes between man and nature and a structural analysis of myth and ritual. Structuralists like Lévi-Strauss acknowledge that preliterate men often organize their understanding of their world according to different principles of organization than do men in modern technological societies. The point that they stress is simply the fact that preliterate people do *organize* and *structure* their beliefs and in that sense exhibit logical and rational thought, even though their structures may be very different from our own.

We conclude then that the work of structuralists like Lévi-Strauss has provided important support for the thesis that all men, whether preliterate or modern, religious or secular, use their symbolic media according to patterns that exhibit order and a precise sense of relationship between clearly distinguished parts. We have seen how an apparently irrational sequence of events like the story of Asdiwal reveals on closer scrutiny a complex set of very exact structures in intricate relation with one another. We should never assume in advance that any set of religious forms is the expression of blind emotion or a vague imagination oblivious to logic and order.

It is true that many problems remain which cannot be considered at this introductory level. In places Lévi-Strauss asserts that all men reveal a common and universal mental structure that is revealed in each of their symbolic expressions. For our purposes this question can be left open as a matter for further study. It is sufficient here if we adopt the methodical maxim that in examining any piece of religious symbolism we will look for underlying patterns of meaning. If we adopt this heuristic principle, we will be constantly surprised to find that ideas, images, and tales, which at first glance appear to be quite fantastic, often disclose underlying meanings that are important to the culture concerned and often have relevance to our own as well.

12. Ibid.

PRIMITIVE RELIGIOUS SYSTEMS: THE NUER AND THE DINKA

The poet William Wordsworth once observed that "we murder to dissect." In the preceding two chapters we have looked in a piece-meal fashion at various rituals, myths, and symbols. In doing so, we have made useful discoveries about how religion functions in concrete circumstances. At the same time, we have not yet considered the manner in which these parts interact with one another to form a unified whole. In this chapter we shall look at an example of how a religious system operates as a totality in the life of a given society. We shall take our example from among the many primitive societies still in existence.

THE NATURE OF PRIMITIVE SOCIETIES

However, we must first define what we mean by a "primitive society." The term refers to a specific kind of social structure with distinctive characteristics. Primitive societies are small and originally isolated from larger civilizations. Kinship structures are usually a dominant factor in their social organization.

Furthermore, there is relative absence of social *differentiation*. As Marshall Sahlins puts it:

> The tribal structure is generalized; in this lies its primitiveness. It lacks an independent economic sector or a separate religious organization, let alone a special political mechanism. In a tribe, these are not so much different institutions as they are different functions of the same institutions: different things a lineage, for instance, may do. Holding an estate in land, the lineage appears as an economic entity; feuding it is a political group; sacrificing to the ancestors, a ritual congregation.[1]

1. Marshall Sahlins, *Tribesmen*, Englewood Cliffs, N. J., Prentice-Hall, 1968, p. 15.

Other characteristics of primitive societies are the prominence of religion in the structure as a whole; the lack of "advanced" technology, especially the skill of writing; the absence of cities. Such societies have existed since Neolithic times and before; they continue to survive in North and South America, Africa, the Andaman Islands, Australia, and the islands of the Pacific, but seem to be fast dying out under impact with the larger, technically advanced, socially differentiated civilizations.

Recently many anthropologists have warned against the negative connotations of the term "primitive" which seem to suggest inferiority.[2] This is an important point and involves a question of attitude as much as the use of a specific term. The first representatives of "civilization" (explorers, traders, and missionaries) looked down on the "primitive" societies they invaded. Since then, we have come to appreciate the cultural achievement of peoples who have worked out impressive ways of living with one another that are different, but not inferior, to those of civilization. If we believe this, we will use the word "primitive" with no sense of devaluation. If we do not, then any alternative term we substitute will soon become infected with the same negative feeling. For example, many have suggested using the descriptive term "preliterate" for the societies we have described. But if we have a bias in favor of writing and a disdain for the "ignorance" of those without that skill, then this term will soon possess the same difficulties as "primitive." The solution is not to change the word, but to enlarge our sympathetic understanding of cultures different from our own.

NUERLAND AND
DINKALAND:
EXAMPLES OF RELIGIOUS
BELIEF SYSTEMS

There is a danger that reference to "primitive society" as a collective noun may obscure the diversity and heterogeneity existing among primitive societies in different parts of the world. Just as it is more accurate to say that we are studying religions, rather than religion, so we must learn how to study the *religions* of primitive societies, not a single homogeneous entity called "primitive religion." The religious forms of tribal societies differ in various parts of the world.

We propose to sketch briefly the religious beliefs of two geographically contiguous societies: the Nuer and the Dinka. These two cultures are not "typical" of African tribal societies as a whole. On the contrary, their social forms and religious practices have features peculiar to themselves. However, they will serve our purpose here, which is to look at a particular primitive religious system *in concreto*.

The Nuer are a cattle-herding people dwelling in the swamps and savannah of the southern Egyptian Sudan. Dinkaland is to the south and west of Nuerland in the swamps of the central Nile Basin. We are fortunate to have detailed accounts of the religions of these societies by trained and highly gifted anthropologists. E. E. Evans-

2. Ashley Montague, ed., *The Concept of the Primitive*, New York, Free Press, 1968.

Pritchard has provided us with a penetrating study of the Nuer, and Godfrey Lienhardt has done the same for the Dinka.[3] In this chapter we will follow their accounts closely and reproduce their descriptions of certain beliefs, rites, and myths in detail. This is because we now want to obtain a three-dimensional picture of what religious actions are like in their concrete manifestations. The reader is asked to attend closely to the details. It is in them that the life and vitality of what we mean by religion is present.

We will seek to examine the religious systems of these people in both synthetic and analytical terms. On the one hand, we want to see the system as a dynamic whole (synthesis); at the same time we want to become more self-consciously aware of its many interacting parts (analysis). Thus the various *elements* of religious systems— beliefs, rituals, sacred forms and objects, religious functionaries, ethos or life-style, basic thought forms—will all be considered through concrete examples.

Nuer religion refers to spirits (*kuth*), the plural of the word for spirit (*kwoth*). These spirits fall into two main categories, spirits of the above (*kuth nhial*) and spirits of the below or of the earth (*kuth piny*). The spirits of the above include powerful beings of the air such as Deng, Teny, and Wiu. These spirit beings may on occasion attach themselves to a certain family or individual. It is believed that they can enter into a person and possess his mind either temporarily or permanently.

A RELIGIOUS BELIEF SYSTEM

The spirits of the earth include totemic spirits, nature spirits, and fetishes. A totem is an animal, plant, or physical object which is identified with a particular clan. Nuer believe that various spirits are associated with these totemic figures. Nature spirits called *bieli* are inferior powers connected with natural phenomena like a meteorite, a river, or fire. Fetish spirits are associated with particular physical substances like a piece of wood. The word "fetish" has been used by some observers to refer to a physical object which primitive people supposedly venerate in itself as an ultimate object of worship. In the case of the Nuer, certain substances are called "medicine which talks," but it turns out that Nuer believe that a fetish spirit of the earth is in the material, and it is this which they respect, not the substance alone.

We have not yet touched on the heart of Nuer belief. To do this, we must look again at the crucial word *spirit*. The Nuer use this word as a singular proper noun (*Kwoth*) to refer to the Spirit who has created the world and determines the occurrence of all events. Evans-Pritchard translates the word as "God." To avoid a too hasty identification with the Western biblical use of that name, we may prefer to consider it here as Spirit.

Spirit is closely associated with the sky and although believed to be everywhere, he is also located in a special way in the heav-

3. E. E. Evans-Pritchard, *Nuer Religion*, Oxford, Clarendon Press, 1956. Godfrey Lienhardt, *Divinity and Experience*, Oxford, Clarendon Press, 1961.

ens. Nuer say he is in this respect "like wind" and "like air." He is often called *Kwoth Neahl* (Spirit of the Sky) or *Kwoth a nhial* (Spirit who is in the Sky). Spirit is a living person (*ran*) and is addressed as "grandfather," "ancestor," or as "Spirit who created my ancestor." He sees and hears all that happens, can be angry and can love; however, he is not anthropomorphic in the sense of possessing a human body; says Evans-Pritchard, "I have never heard Nuer suggest that he has human form." On the other hand Lienhardt records an instance where a Dinka claimed to have seen his corresponding deity who looked to him like "an old man, with a red and blue pied body and a white head." [4]

Spirit upholds what might be called the moral order of the world. Nuer are aware that good conduct is not necessarily followed immediately by happy situations, nor wicked acts by retribution. In the long run, however, they believe that Spirit sees to it that a kind of correlation between goodness and happiness and the obverse does take place. No man can avoid all misfortunes, for some are a part of the natural situation, to be accepted as the will of Spirit. But special misfortunes come to a man as the result of a "fault" (*duer*), as when he breaks a divinely sanctioned interdiction, wrongs another, or fails in his obligations to spiritual beings and the ghosts of his kith and kin. If a man remains in the right, i.e., avoids "fault," Spirit will probably protect him from dire troubles and woes. However, Spirit cannot be controlled or compelled by any particular ritual or action. The final decisions about a man's destiny belong to Spirit, who in the end is always in the right.

The Dinka use different semantic terms for their spirits but exhibit an almost identical pattern with the Nuer. According to Lienhardt, "the word which any inquirer into Dinka religion will first and most frequently hear is *nhialic.*" This is the Dinka word for sky; in Dinka religion it becomes the name of the mighty being who is addressed as "creator" (*aciek*) and "my father" (*wa*) and to whom prayers and sacrifice are offered.

Lienhardt suggests translating *nhialic* when used this way as *Divinity*, a word with more flexibility for shades of nuance than the word "God." Divinity is *jok*, a word which can be translated "spirit" but which Lienhardt calls "power." According to the Dinka, there are many powers and *yeeth* is a collective name for "powers which are related to people." They can be called divinities. Lienhardt notes two major kinds of divinities among the Dinka: clan divinities, which are connected specifically with particular lineage groups, and free divinities, which sometimes appear to individuals irrespective of their clan affiliations.

We may ask a similar question of both Dinka religion and Nuer religion concerning the relation between the Nuer Spirit and the spirits and between the Dinka Divinity and the many powers. In both cases we are provided with a religious pattern that in some respects seems to be monotheistic, i.e., oriented

4. *Divinity and Experience*, p. 46.

toward a single god. In other respects the patterns seem to be polytheistic, i.e., oriented around belief in many gods; there are also suggestions of *pantheistic* conceptions, i.e., beliefs that divine reality is an animating power interpenetrating and infusing all beings and entities of the natural world.

As an example of this ambiguity, Leinhardt tells us, "All Dinka assert that Divinity is one, *nhialic ee tok.*" Nevertheless, it is also possible to say of each special divinity, "it is Divinity" (*ee nhialic*). Lienhardt declares: "This unity and multiplicity of Divinity causes no difficulty in the context of Dinka language and life, but it is impossible entirely to avoid the logical and semantic problems which arise when Dinka statements bearing upon it are translated together into English." [5] The same ambiguity is present in Nuer expressions. On the one hand, we have here a clear example of a polytheistic hierarchy of divine spirits. Spirit is the father of the greater spirits of the air, and the lesser of them are said to be children of his sons, of his lineage. The totemic spirits are children of his daughters, a lower order on the hierarchical scale. The fetishes are lower yet, children of the daughters of the air spirit *Denq*.[6]

However, Evans-Pritchard insists that the Nuer takes these schemes in a metaphoric sense. The actual relation between Spirit and the spirits is more complex. Evans-Pritchard approaches the question largely through attention to the linguistic pattern involved, which is curious. *Kwoth* is not a proper name, but the word is used to refer to the creator of the world who has no name but is simply the "Spirit in the sky." The same word is then used to refer to the other spirits of the air and earth. Yet the "Spirit in the sky" does not belong to a class in common with the other spirits. Nuer either speak collectively of "the spirits" or singularly of the Spirit in the sky, but the latter is not included as one member of the former. In other words, Spirit is not one of the spirits, but rather the spirits are special forms or "refractions" of Spirit. This might be called pantheism, but Evans-Pritchard finally decides that the term "modalism" is more useful at this point. He writes:

It follows from the conception of God as Spirit that though he is figured in many diverse figures he can be thought of both as each and as all alike and one. But if we say that in spite of the many different spirits Spirit is one and that Nuer religion is in this sense monotheistic we have to add that it is also modalistic. Spirit, though one, is differently thought of with regard to different effects and relations.[7]

Since God is Kwoth *in the sense of Spirit, the other spirits, whilst distinct with regard to one another, are all, being also* Kwoth, *thought of as being of the same nature as God. Each of them,*

5. Ibid., p. 56.
6. *Nuer Religion*, p. 119.
7. Ibid., p. 316.

*that is to say, is God regarded in a particular way; and it may
help us if we think of the particular spirits as figures or representations or refractions of God in relation to particular activities,
events, persons, and groups.*[8]

The Nuer thus believe that an encounter with a specific spirit in a
religious rite is in the end an encounter with Spirit. There is a distinction between Spirit and spirits but there is also a fundamental
unity. The Nuer do not claim to be able to define what Spirit is, but
they believe that it is the ultimate power inhabiting the world
"above" and that all creatures, whether spirits or human beings, depend on him for their existence in the world.

SOULS, GHOSTS, AND LIFE AFTER DEATH

The Nuer have a number of different words to specify various aspects of the human being. *Ring* is the word for flesh, the corporal
body. *Yiegh* means life or breath. It is the animating principle which
on death returns to Spirit. *Ran* is the person, primarily in his social
setting as determined by kinship relationship. To make this clear,
we might note that identical twins have a common or single *ran*. Finally, the word *tie* is best translated as "soul." It embraces the intellectual and moral faculties and often refers to a man's "clever-
ness" or "wisdom." It is the center of his personality both as an
individual and social entity.

Care should be taken not to force on these conceptions a greater
sense of division than is actually meant. To judge that the Nuer has
separated the person into a number of distinct entities—*tie, joagh,
ran, tiep*—is as misleading as to judge that modern Westerners
have divided the person up into distinct entities called self, personality, ego, intellect, life, soul, spirit, mind, and consciousness. These
terms are used by us in different ways to refer to various functions
of the human being, according to the context specified. The same is
true of the Nuer, who have words to express wholeness as well as
distinction: *Pwong* is the whole creature, the total organism; *ran* is
the total personality.

Nuer believe that at death the physical flesh goes into the ground,
but a part of the person, the ghost (*joagh*), continues to exist. The
Nuer have not worked out the details of their beliefs about the final
state of human existence after death into a unified system. Two different sets of statements are often made. One is that when people
die, "they have become ghosts." The other is that the dead person
"has joined Spirit" and "His soul has gone above, [only] his flesh
was buried." The distinction operating in the Nuer mind seems to
be between souls that still retain the possibility of returning to the
living as ghosts in dreams or haunting them in other ways and souls
that are completely cut off from the living, since they have returned
to Spirit as their final destination.

In this connection an unusual and dramatic incident is recorded
by Evans-Pritchard. In western Nuerland he met "an unhappy-look-
ing man of unkempt appearance." This man had gone on a journey

8. Ibid., p. 107.

years before and after a long time the villagers received news of his death and a mortuary ceremony was held for him. The news proved to be false; the man returned, but he was declared by the villagers to be a "living ghost." It was affirmed that "his soul was cut off. His soul went with the soul of the (sacrificed) ox together. His flesh alone remains standing." In other words, he was believed to still possess body and life, but to be without soul. This meant he had lost his social role and was forbidden to participate in sacrificial rituals. One native explained: "He lives in our village . . . but we do not count him a member of it because he is dead. The mortuary ceremony has been held for him." [9]

An important point to realize about the religion of the Nuer is that although they definitely believe in the continued existence of the soul after death, the focus of their concern is with the ongoing life of the community and with the existence of the dead insofar as it affects the living. Many rituals, for example, have as their purpose the assurance that ghosts will continue on the way to their final destination and not return to haunt or otherwise afflict the living. At a mortuary ceremony the ghost is addressed: "Turn away! Turn thy face away into the bush! Do not look at us again! We have given thee thine own things, but then leave us alone!" [10] Thus Raymond Firth observes "primitive communities have no great *concern* about the fate of their own souls." He goes on to note: "It is rather as a framework for activity in *this* world and for positive experience in *life* that concepts about the continuity and fate of the soul are developed rather than as protection against death . . . the concern for freedom of action of the living is most marked." [11]

This judgment is true of the Nuer. As Evans-Pritchard puts it: "They are not interested in the survival of the individual as a ghost, but in the survival of the social personality in the name." Their desire is to participate in a lineage having roots in the distant past and which will continue on earth after the person's death. Hence, if a man has died without children, it is the duty of his next of kin to marry a woman in the dead man's name before he takes a wife in his own. In theory, every man must have at least one son to form a link in the chain of genealogical descent. Souls after death continue the lineage patterns of the living and their relations among themselves as dead are similar to those that pertained while alive. The living and the dead thus comprise a single cosmic pattern of social existence.

In an earlier chapter we stressed the importance of ritual in understanding religion. In the case of the Nuer and the Dinka, the texture and tone of their beliefs only come truly alive when we consider them in relation to their central rituals—in both cases acts of animal sacrifice.

RITUAL SACRIFICE

9. Ibid., p. 153.
10. Ibid., p. 149.
11. Raymond Firth, "The Fate of the Soul," *Tikopia Ritual and Belief,* London, G. Allen, 1967, p. 334.

A Nuer sacrifice: final invocation over slain victim. (*From E. E. Evans-Pritchard,* Nuer Religion; *courtesy of the Clarendon Press, Oxford.*)

Animals such as goats and ewes, or grain products like maize and millet, are offered in Nuer sacrifices. However, the principal sacrificial object is the bull or ox. Almost all sacrifices follow a common sequence. The first act is the *pivot,* driving a stake into the ground and tethering the animal to it. Then takes place the *buk,* the rubbing of ashes on the animal as an act of consecration. This is followed by the *lam,* or invocation. The officiant, holding his spear in his right hand, speaks to Spirit over the consecrated victim. Finally is the *kam yang,* the giving or offering of the animal. The ox is speared on the right side so expertly it usually falls to the right side as intended a few seconds after the thrust. Afterward the meat of the animal is divided up and eaten by the community.

Sacrifices occur on two sets of occasions. Often they are attempts to prevent or alleviate some misfortune that may befall a person, usually as the result of fault. These can be called piacular sacrifices. Second, a sacrifice may accompany a rite of passage like an initiation or wedding. These can be called confirmatory sacrifices, since they have the effect of validating and celebrating the particular act in question.

These two kinds of sacrificial acts reveal a striking example of an ambivalence common in many religious forms. Confirmatory sacrifices invoke the presence of Spirit and are, in that sense, a desire for communion. At the same time, piacular sacrifices have the idea of ridding man of Spirit's presence, which is disturbing and dangerous. If man has done wrong, Spirit is manifested in some affliction that has beset him. The sacrifice causes Spirit to depart and leave man to his ordinary course of life.

We cannot appreciate the full significance of this sacrificial act until we understand the importance of cattle to Nuer and Dinka. The relation between Nuer and cattle is personal, intimate, profound. First of all, these people are dependent on the milk of their herds for life itself. The land in which they live exhibits a harsh environment and is poor in natural resources. In this situation a condition of mutual dependence exists between man and cattle, since it is not likely that either would long survive without the other.

Furthermore, a man's social identity is determined through cattle. The Dinka words for basic social groupings refer equally to groupings of men and to groupings of cattle. Each clan has an ox name. In many sacrifices the meat of the animal is divided according to lineage groupings. The owning of a herd or possessing rights to a herd determines social status, prestige, and power in the community.

Personal identity is also related to cattle. Upon passing through the rite of passage from boy to man, the initiate is given an ox name and an ox from the herd, which becomes his own. The man is identified with his ox and it becomes his friend and companion. Dinka explicitly conceive their own lives and the lives of cattle in some ways on the same model. Men imitate cattle. "A characteristic sight in western Dinkaland is that of a young man with his arms curved above his head, posturing either at a dance or for his own enjoyment when he is alone with his little herd." [12]

It is also important to realize that cattle are never killed and eaten for any other purpose than sacrifice, except in times of great distress as when famine and drought are threatening the community.

Nuer explain the meaning of sacrifice in a number of different ways. They often call a sacrifice a *kok,* which contains the notion of a debt, a ransom, a price paid. The image behind this idea suggests a commercial transaction. On the other hand, the word *lor* is also used to describe sacrifice; it literally means "to go to meet" and has the idea of honoring the person concerned. Another word, *kier,* conveys the sense of an act of expiation, whereby the anger of Spirit, aroused by some human "fault," has been appeased. The word *col,* in this connection, has the notion of reparation, whereby an injury done another is paid for or indemnified.

Evans-Pritchard judges that the basic idea operating in Nuer sacrifice is substitution, *vita pro vita.* The life of the ox is given to Spirit. But the life of the ox is a substitute for the life of the owner of the ox. The Nuer has so identified his own life with the ox that one can serve as the substitute for the other. In the sacrificial rite, the man has given Spirit his own self in the form of the ox. In return, Spirit may confirm the validity of a certain ceremony, forgive a transgression, according to the request accompanying the act. Through sacrifice the human life of the Nuer and Dinka achieves a strong sense of identification with the ultimate reality of Spirit or Divinity. The ritual of sacrifice is thus an act through which Dinka

12. *Divinity and Experience,* p. 16.

and Nuer understand the meaning of their world and their own place within it. It is the central focus of their life as a whole.

THE SACRED SPEAR

A religious system makes use of a variety of symbolic tools. Not only myths and rituals, but symbolic objects play an important role in expressing religious meaning. Among the Nuer the spear assumes a place of special importance.

The spear is to the Nuer both a tool and a weapon which he keeps constantly with him and never tires of sharpening and polishing. It is treated almost like an animate object for "it is an extension and external symbol of the right hand, which stands for the strength, vitality, and virtue of the person." It is a projection of the self, so when a man hurls his spear he cries out either "my right hand" or the name of the ox with which he is identified. The spear plays a great role in religious rituals. At initiation, the boy is invested with a special fighting spear as well as an ox so that the two are deeply connected with his own adult identity. In sacrifice, a spear is brandished in the right hand as the officiant walks up and down past the victim.

Evans-Pritchard points out that the spear names and actual existing spears in the tribe assume an essential symbolic function.

> The virtue is in the idea of "the spear of our fathers," not in any material clan relic. Consequently, in invocations any spear will serve the purpose of the rite and represent that of the ancestor of the clan and hence symbolize the clan as a whole. Any spear will do, but . . . there must be a spear; and when Nuer sitting in my tent recounted to me what is said in invocations they gestured with their right hands as though they had spears in them, for they found it difficult to speak the words without the gestures, just as in recounting what is said in prayers (pal) they found it difficult to do so without moving outstretched hands up and down.[13]

In the Nuer relationship with the spear we see another example of the function of the expressive symbol to the Nuer. The spear combines aspects of personal and social life with a feeling for ancestral ties and a sense of transcendent power on which human life depends. It is a single compelling form in which idea and gesture have become one.

RELIGIOUS FUNCTIONARIES

A religious system is not a constellation of beliefs and rituals floating around in an abstract and ethereal realm of ideas. A religion is enacted by concrete men. Hence the religious functionary—the personage who assumes a given religious role within a certain community—becomes important. One meaningful way of studying a

13. *Nuer Religion*, pp. 240–241.

religious system is through the kinds of religious figures who maintain the practices in the midst of the community.

Evans-Pritchard designates two religious functionaries as having special importance in Nuer religion. The first is the *Kuaar,* which can be translated as "priest." Many sacrifices are performed by the head of a given clan or kinship group; but for sacrifices involving the breaking of some divine interdiction, it is considered desirable to seek the services of a *Kuaar twac,* "priest of the leopard skin." For example, if one man has slain another, to avoid being slain by the dead man's kin he may stay for a time in the home of the priest, who is considered sacred, and whose environs are consequently considered a sanctuary where violence cannot take place. The priest will help the guilty man make his compensation to the aggrieved relatives and also officiate in a sacrificial ritual whereby the guilty man can come to terms with Spirit who is offended by the act.

Another kind of religious functionary in Nuer society is the *Gwan Kwoth,* the "possessor of spirit." Evans-Pritchard translates this term by the word "prophet." It is believed that the "possessor of spirit" has been seized by Spirit and has literally become Spirit's mouthpiece. He enters into ecstatic states of consciousness in which he leaps about and makes utterances that represent messages from Spirit. Ordinary people may on occasion have such an experience, but it is only when the soul of man has become permanently seized and transformed by Spirit that he is called a prophet. Among the Dinka such a person is called *ran nhialic,* "man of divinity." Because of the possession, they are believed to have unusual powers. The prophets offer divine instructions to assist in warfare; they perform healings and the exorcism of bad spirits. They also predict the future and can offer advice helpful to the asker in working out his personal problem.

The prophet is evidently a much later development in Dinka religion than is the priest. People feel ambivalent toward him because Spirit is believed to be directly present in him; although Spirit can help man, his presence is also dangerous, so the prophet is one who is both sought out and avoided.

These two figures in Dinka and Nuer religion represent two religious roles found in many forms of religion. They appear in Old Testament religion and Max Weber has used the terms to indicate two ideal types of religious figures. Evans-Pritchard sketches their differences in terms of Nuer religion as follows:

> *The priest is a traditional functionary of Nuer society; the prophet is a recent development; the priest has an appointed sacrificial role in certain situations of the social life, particularly in homicide and blood-feud; the prophet's functions are indeterminate. The priest's powers are transmitted by descent from the first priest—a social heritage; the prophet's powers are charismatic—an individual inspiration. The virtue of the priest resides in his office; that of the prophet in himself. . . . But the most outstanding con-*

ceptual difference is that whereas in the priest man speaks to God, in the prophet God, in one or other of his hypostases, speaks to man. The priest stands on the earth and looks to the sky. Heavenly beings descend from the sky and fill the prophets.[14]

Considered as ideal types, the priest has an essentially conservative role in maintaining the rituals of the cult and the harmonious life of the community, whereas the prophet can be more revolutionary and innovative; the words Spirit speaks through him may generate changes in the patterns of social order or at least introduce some notion to the person that is relevant to him individually without being part of an already existing communal lore. Both priest and prophet have played an important role in the history of religion.

MYTH AND LIFE-STYLE

We have already noted the important part that myth plays in primitive religions. Among the Dinka is an interesting myth about the origin of the present human world.

A myth tells how Divinity (and the sky) and men (and the earth) were originally contiguous; the sky then lay just above the earth. They were connected by a rope, stretched parallel to the earth and at the reach of a man's outstretched arm above it. By means of this rope men could clamber at will to Divinity. At this time there was no death. Divinity granted one grain of millet a day to the first man and woman, and this satisfied their needs. They were forbidden to grow or pound more. Divinity here clearly emerges as a person, with the attributes of father and creator, and conceptually distinct from the observable sky; in this context we can thus refer to Divinity with the personal pronoun, as "he."
The first human beings, usually called Garang and Abuk, living on earth had to take care when they were doing their little planting or pounding, lest a hoe or a pestle should strike Divinity, but one day the woman "because she was greedy" (in this context any Dinka would view her "greed" indulgently) decided to plant (or pound) more than the permitted grain of millet. In order to do so she took one of the long-handled hoes (or pestles) which the Dinka now use. In raising this pole to pound or cultivate, she struck Divinity who withdrew, offended, to his present great distance from the earth, and sent a small blue bird (the colour of the sky) called atoc to sever the rope which had previously given men access to the sky and to him. Since that time the country has been "spoilt," for men have to labour for the food they need, and are often hungry. They can no longer as before freely reach Divinity, and they suffer sickness and death, which thus accompany their abrupt separation from Divinity.[15]

This myth reveals a theme found in numerous creation stories in the religions of tribal societies and archaic civilizations. In the

14. Ibid., p. 304.
15. *Divinity and Experience*, pp. 33–34.

Dinka story a rope unites heaven and earth. In other stories it is a ladder ("The Story of Asdiwal" in the preceding chapter), a pole, a sacred tree. These sacred stories reveal a common pattern that describes a primordial condition in which heaven and earth are originally connected (sometimes intermingled) before a radical separation of them brings about the present human condition.

Another Dinka myth of some importance explains the origin of the priestly clan of the spear masters. The myth tells of Aiwel who was born of a union between a mortal woman and a Power of the river named Malengdit. On reaching maturity, he returned one day from the river with an ox of every known color, but predominantly the color of rain clouds. Aiwel took the ox's name—Longar—as his own.

The central action of the myth deals with a curious set of circumstances that is described with variations in different forms of the myth. The basic situation finds Longar on one side of a river and the people attempting to cross the river and join him. Longar stands at the side of the river and spears each person who attempts to mount the banks on his side.

Lienhardt points out that Longar is "an essentially mysterious figure to the Dinka themselves." They have no real answer as to the reason for his hostility, other than it is as much a part of his nature to do so, as is his subsequent kindness. When disaster strikes, the Dinka say *"acie nhialic,"* i.e., "is it not Divinity?" From this point of view Longar is as motiveless as nature itself.

In a sense Longar seems to represent the point of contact between man and the mysterious Power on whom his existence depends. As one Dinka observed: "Longar was like a Power (*jok*) and he was like a man. It was he who was the first of all to be created. He had just come from Divinity's hand. He was at the head (source) of all life. He wanted to try everything, to test everything." [16] Through Longar, Divinity and man meet and the nature of man is tested, formed, developed. The present condition of man grows out of this primordial encounter.

Various forms of the myth then explain slightly different ways in which Longar is changed from an enemy into a friend of the different clans of the spear masters. One interesting version is as follows:

> Longar called the people, and called upon them all in turn to repeat his invocations (gam lung de); as soon as they did so, they died. And there was a man called Adheou, the youngest son created in the river, who said he would try to repeat the invocations of Longar. Ajiek tried to dissuade him, telling him that he would surely die, but Adheou began to repeat the invocations and did not die.

Longar was baffled and he thought of several other trials. Always Adheou prevailed. Finally Longar said:

16. Ibid., p. 182.

A Dinka spear master's shrine and spears. (*From Godfrey Lienhardt,* Divinity and Experience; *courtesy of the Clarendon Press, Oxford.*)

"Adheou, you have exhausted me. You shall be the foremost of the people to whom I have given my flesh, and even though I invoke against you myself, I shall not prevail." The people stayed thus. The land was good and well-ordered. It was so. It was great Longar; he divided (shared out) the fishing-spears, and he shared out the flesh.[17]

The myth of Longar and Adheou provides an important expression of the ethos or life style of the Dinka and the Nuer. Clifford Geertz defines ethos of a people as "the tone, character, and quality of their life, its moral and aesthetic style and mood; it is the underlying attitude toward themselves and their world that life reflects." [18]

The two myths of the Dinka which we have considered express a life style in which humble acceptance and self-assertion are combined. On the one hand, the Dinka live in a world which is largely beyond their control. At the same time it is only by acts of self-assertion combined with underlying respect before the mysterious power of Divinity that a human society can be achieved.

17. Ibid., pp. 180–181.
18. Clifford Geertz, "Ethos, World-View and the Analysis of Sacred Symbols," *Antioch Review* (Winter 1957–1958), p. 421.

Both Nuer and Dinka stress the basic right of Spirit or Divinity to direct all events of life as he chooses. Thus the Nuer stress humility before Spirit and the virtue of accepting his will without complaint. They say, "we, all of us, have the nature of ants in that we are very tiny in respect to Spirit." However, it would be a serious mistake to conclude that this humility leads to a kind of servility and general passivity before the course of nature. On the contrary, Evans-Pritchard tells us that the Nuer display a proud, almost provocative, and towards strangers even insulting, bearing to men." [19]

The sense of human self-assertion comes out most strongly in the myth of Longar which we have also considered. As Lienhardt points out:

> We see that what appears in all the versions given is original opposition between leaders of the Dinka, in which some wrest strength from an original master of the fishing-spear, who is at the same time a human being and a Power, and receive a mandate from him. The man who causes him to share his powers is one who acts intelligently to outwit and oppose him, and finally propitiates him. The themes of human initiative, and propitiation, appear similarly in the effective regulation of human relations with the free-divinities. The men who in these myths eventually save their people from the human power, Longar, are those who act, with force and intelligence but, finally, with respect.[20]

In this last sentence is stated the two poles of the Nuer and Dinka life-style. On the one hand human "force" is approved; man must strive to maintain himself in a universe in which the benign and the dangerous elements are intermixed. At the same time he must inculcate a proper "respect" for the ultimate power on which he depends. The Nuer call this attitude *theok*, or, in its verbal form, *thek*. *Thek* conveys the attitude of "deference, constraint, modesty or shyness" with which one should approach a totemic object, treat certain humans, like a wife's parents, or treat divine interdictions and ritual acts.[21] Lienhardt defines *thek* (the same word is used by both Dinka and Nuer) as "a compound of behavior which shows inaggressiveness and deference to its object, and of behavior which shows esteem for it." [22] Respect is shown to clan divinities during the sacrifices in their honor. Sacrificial oxen are treated with respect and are declared to be *mac*, i.e., dedicated for sacrifice to a particular divinity. "Teasing, joking, and horseplay, which are not inappropriate between those who regard themselves as familiar equals and perhaps in some sense rivals, are improper between those who practise *thek*." [23] The attitude of respect is clearly related to what other scholars call the sense of the sacred.

We may summarize the life-style of the Nuer and Dinka by ob-

19. *Nuer Religion*, p. 12.
20. *Divinity and Experience*, pp. 184–185.
21. *Nuer Religion*, p. 180.
22. *Divinity and Experience*, p. 126.
23. Ibid., p. 125.

serving that it seeks to combine the vitality of human assertiveness with the sense of respect for the power and mystery exhibited in the universe. A man who does not show respect for the divine interdictions and rules is "crazy" (*yong*) because he loses both support of his kin and the favor of Spirit. Human pride and respect, then, are not mutually exclusive, but complementary poles that together enable man to make his way in a baffling but also wondrous world.

CONCLUSION   We have now considered a number of ways in which religion can be studied. We have considered the task of adequate *description* and its relation to the task of *interpretation*. Can anything more be said? Can we offer any further *explanation* of what happens in the religious activity of mankind?

An explanation involves the relating of the questioned phenomenon to some wider context of meaning which for us seems to be satisfactorily understood, and, at least for the moment, not itself demanding an explanation. For example, if a person drops to his knees, I might ask "why?" i.e., request an explanation. A curt "why not?" will not satisfy me; I feel that this behavior is not understandable and acceptable in itself, because a man usually stands, sits, or lies down, rather than rests on his knees. I may then be told that he has dropped a coin and is looking for it (economic explanation), is playing a game (social explanation), is looking at a pattern in the rug (aesthetic explanation), or is praying (religious explanation). Whichever of these proves to be correct may serve as an explanation since it has integrated a puzzling fact into a wider context that is for me understandable. However, if that wider context is itself puzzling, then the offered explanation requires a still wider context of meaning into which it can be placed. Thus the fact the man is praying explains why he is on his knees, but now I ask in turn, "why is he praying?"

How are we to answer this question? The beginning student is urged to keep in mind the complexity of religious symbolism and to avoid premature reductionism and oversimplification. As Mircea Eliade observes:

> There is no such thing as a "pure" religious fact. Such a fact is always also a historical, sociological, cultural, and psychological fact, to name only the most important contexts. If the historian of religions does not always insist on this multiplicity of meanings, it is mainly because he is supposed to concentrate on the religious signification of his documents. The confusion starts when only one aspect of religious life is accepted as primary and meaningful, and the other aspects or functions are regarded as secondary or even illusory.[24]

But if we do not reduce religion to a concern with some natural, psychological, or social dimension of life, what categories remain in

24. Mircea Eliade, *The Quest*, Chicago, The University of Chicago Press, 1969, p. 19.

which to specify its own autonomous focus? Mircea Eliade suggests that the notion of sacred existence as distinct from the ordinary and mundane form of life may be useful. Religious symbols seem to evoke a sense of sacred reality in some form. The participant feels that he is in the presence of that which is awesome, mysterious, of overwhelming value. How are we to describe this experience of *hierophany,* i.e., the manifestation of sacred presence? We can speak of a sacred *world* to which religious symbols relate the user as a higher *realm* or *being* in which the perplexities and distortions of this life are finally resolved. Or we can speak of a sacred *modality* in which religious symbols provide the religious man with a special way or mode of *being in this world* through sacred rite. On this view religious myths and rituals help men to achieve a sacred style and stance in which his life finds ultimate equilibrium and meaning.

If we ask the Nuer and Dinka themselves for an explanation of what they are doing in their religious practices, they are inclined to be cautious and circumspect. Many Western observers attribute to the primitive religious mind a greater cognitive pride and presumption than it actually possesses.

Evans-Pritchard writes:

> *If we seek for . . . a statement of what Spirit is thought to be like in itself, we seek of course in vain. Nuer do not claim to know. They say that they are merely* doar, *simple people, and how can simple people know about such matters? What happens in the world is determined by Spirit and Spirit can be influenced by prayer and sacrifice. This much they know, but no more; and they say, very sensibly, that since the European is so clever perhaps he can tell them the answer to the question he asks.*[25]

This polite request of the Nuer can be, and has been, answered in many ways. A Christian theologian may be impressed by the similarity between Nuer patterns and the Old Testament. He may then offer a theological explanation: *Kwoth* is a reflection of the Old Testament God in the hearts of primitive man and an indication of a natural revelation. On this view Nuer religion has been *explained* by relating it to the context of a religion more familiar to the theologian. Again, a Vedanta philosopher from India may say that, on the contrary, *Kwoth,* with its many forms and modalistic refractions, more clearly indicates an awareness of the eternal invisible Reality called Brahman, of whom all forms of the visible world are manifestations.

On the other hand, secular philosophers may rather put the Nuer religion into some more familiar natural context. A follower of Freud might argue that while Nuer religion purports to be about "Spirit," it is really explained as the human projection of infantile needs for security and a protecting father into images of supportive divine beings. A follower of Durkheim may rather feel that the evidence has clearly shown that Nuer religion is about "society," which is symbolized by the relationships among divine beings.

25. *Nuer Religion,* pp. 315–316.

Evans-Pritchard ends his study of Nuer religion by letting the religious phenomenon itself have, so to say, the last word. He writes in conclusion:

We can, therefore, say no more than that Spirit is an intuitive apprehension, something experienced in response to certain situations but known directly only to the imagination and not to the senses. Nuer religious conceptions are properly speaking not concepts but imaginative constructions. If we regard only what happens in sacrifice before the eyes it may seem to be a succession of senseless, and even cruel and repulsive, acts, but when we reflect on their meaning we perceive that they are a dramatic representation of a spiritual experience. What this experience is the anthropologist cannot for certain say. Experiences of this kind are not easily communicated even when people are ready to communicate them and have a sophisticated vocabulary in which to do so. Though prayer and sacrifice are exterior actions, Nuer religion is ultimately an interior state. This state is externalized in rites which we can observe, but their meaning depends finally on an awareness of God and that men are dependent on him and must be resigned to his will.[26]

Whatever may be our personal conclusions about the final impact of religious phenomena, we must take care to avoid simplifications. Religion is a human phenomenon that is complex, intimate, important. It can be studied in an objective manner by human scientific skills that will provide ever more accurate *descriptions* and ever more sensitive *interpretations* of what is occurring. We have argued that agreement among careful investigations is possible at these levels of discourse. However, it is more difficult to agree on final *explanations*. The final explanation of the import and meaning of religious phenomena depends on complex decisions about man and his relation to his world. Each student must decide what best helps him to understand the role that religion finally plays in the drama of human existence.

26. Ibid., pp. 321–322.

THE HISTORICAL FORMS OF RELIGION

In the preceding chapters we have examined examples of religious phenomena primarily from psychological, sociological, and hermeneutical perspectives. However, most comparative questions concerning the relation between a religious form in one tradition and that in another have been deliberately avoided since they become involved in complicated and difficult problems best dealt with in a subsequent course.

The most glaring omission in our account so far has been the lack of a historical approach. The reason is that we have begun our study with a consideration of tribal or preliterate societies. These societies tend to be ahistorical in the sense that they are not oriented toward an interest in the sequences of changes in the life of the society that comprise its history.

Modern Western societies have become acutely aware of the fact that both the worlds of nature and human society are in a continual process of change. We realize that even tribal societies have not existed forever in a static and immutable form, but have gone through various processes of transformation and development. Nevertheless, in a tribal society these changes have been more gradual than in modern societies. Tribal societies tend to orient themselves through symbol and ritual practice toward a view of the world in which change is minimized and the existing society is viewed as a constant form repeating patterns learned in the distant past. As Lévi-Strauss puts it:

Each of these societies considers that its essential and ultimate aim is to persevere in its existing form and carry on as it was es-

tablished by its ancestors, and for the sole reason that it was so fashioned by its ancestors. There is no need for any further justification; "that is how we have always done it" is the reply we receive without fail whenever we ask an informant the reason for a particular custom or institution. The fact that it exists is its only justification. It is legitimate because it has endured.[1]

It is in this sense that we can say that tribal societies are ahistorical and that modern Western societies are historical ones. Lévi-Strauss argues, ". . . whereas so called primitive societies are surrounded by the substance of history and try to remain impervious to it, modern societies interiorize history, as it were, and turn it into the motive power of their development."[2]

In the remainder of this book the approach is primarily historical, though, needless to say, such an approach will also utilize materials gained from psychological, sociological, formal, and hermeneutical perspectives. In this chapter we will take a "bird's-eye" look at the historical panorama as a whole. We will then proceed to examine in more detail the historical development of the great religious systems that are still vital forces in the modern world.

STONE AGE RELIGION
AND THE HUNTERS

According to conservative estimates, man in some form has been present on the earth for at least one million years. About 98 percent of this time consists of an immense period which geologists call the Pleistocene Age and most of which coincides with what archeologists call the Paleolithic (old stone age) period. During this time great glaciers moved south covering great portions of Eurasia and North America, only to recede each time, leaving interglacial interludes in which life adapted to warmer climates could flourish.

The first great cultural event—the use of fire—is lost in the obscurity of the Pleistocene Age. Probably Sinanthropus, or Peking man, had learned how to make use of fire gained from forest conflagrations some 360,000 years ago. We know nothing about his religion, or if he had any. Sometime during the last interglacial period, about 200,000 B.C. or earlier, Neanderthal man appeared in northern Europe.

There are indications that Neanderthal man was concerned with ritual burial of the dead. In one cave, situated in southern France, the remains of two Neanderthal adults and two children have been found. One of the adults, evidently a woman, had been placed in a crouched or flexed position, legs pressed against her body and arms folded upon her breast. In another cave, an adolescent has been buried in a sleeping posture, with his head pillowed on a neat pile of flint fragments. Such arrangements give the impression of ceremonial respect for the dead.

The art of Cro-Magnon man, 30,000–25,000 to 10,000 B.C. has been discovered in a number of caves in southern France and north-

1. G. Charbonnier, *Conversations with Claude Lévi-Strauss*, London, Cape, 1969, pp. 49–50.
2. Ibid., p. 39.

The "Sorcerer" from the cave of Les Trois Frères, France. (Courtesy of the American Museum of Natural History.)

ern Spain. Drawings and paintings were made with ochre on the walls. The fact that some of these representations are placed in interior, not easily accessible, parts of the caves suggests that the enclosures may have been places for religious or magic rites.

In one cave in the Pyrenees is the famous "Sorcerer of Trois Frères." To reach it one has to crawl on his belly through a narrow tube forty or fifty yards long. The figure is two and a half feet high, painted in black, and surrounded by numerous animals. It might represent a controlling god or spirit, or, at the very least, a human sorcerer who has donned ceremonial masks and animal garments.

Scholars continue to debate the meaning of these mysterious paintings. While some have argued that they have a purely decorative function, others argue that they reveal a sense of profound participation between man and the forces of nature, particularly animal life. Some kind of magic or religious relation between men and animals seems to be affirmed.

In general we may assume that paleolithic man probably lived in hunting societies, where the basic means of livelihood is the capturing and killing of wild game. Many primitive hunting societies, like

Two paleolithic bas-reliefs: above, a woman with a drinking horn; below, a spearthrower. (Courtesy of the American Museum of Natural History.)

the Eskimos, Indian tribes of North and South America, Bushmen and pygmies in Africa, etc., are still in existence. Now, it is clearly a dangerous and methodologically unsound practice to infer that the beliefs and practices among living primitive groups were necessarily adhered to by man in prehistoric times. Contemporary primitive societies are the product of much change and transformation. Nevertheless, some continuity between paleolithic hunting societies and modern ones probably exists.

An important figure in hunting societies is the shaman who has the capacity to fall into a trance and receive insight and power that confer on him the role of religious leader in the community. A shaman must go through a terrifying psychological ordeal that accomplishes his initiation into a mode of being and power transcending the everyday life of his fellow tribesmen. Usually, the initiation is described as a long journey during which the shaman fights monsters, descends into nether regions, is "killed" and dismembered. Then the gods restore him to life, sometimes with magic substances placed in his body in lieu of ordinary organs. Finally the shaman goes up to the sky and learns secrets from gods and heroes. All this has occurred in a trance. The shaman is adept in the technique of ecstasy. He returns to the world of his people with powers of healing and the ability to assist them in performing successful hunts.

The religions of hunting societies express a close relationship between the hunters and the animals that they must kill. The killing is a necessity, but the act is done not with hostility or cold mechanical skill; man and animal belong to a common world of dynamic existence and each shares in the being of the other. The killing is then done with reverence and ritual.

The religions of such societies usually contain reference to a high god or some cultic ancestor with great powers. The totem—an animal or other entity with which a clan identifies—is often present. The basic concern is to establish and reinforce a basic connection between man and the animal world through ritual and myth. The religious symbols tend to be theriomorphic, i.e., the gods are represented or symbolized in animal form. There is no doubt that hunter images and insights have provided symbolic materials used in different ways in later religions. One of the roots of religious phenomena is found in the world of the hunters.

NEOLITHIC RELIGION:
PASTORALISTS
AND PLANTERS

The paleolithic culture, covering an epoch of approximately a million years, is followed by a period of mesolithic culture that leads into the important Neolithic time—the new stone age. It should be remembered that we are referring here to periods of culture which have not appeared uniformly and simultaneously throughout the world. In the Near East, the Neolithic period emerges into full flower around 5000 B.C. and lasts until the ensuing iron age civilization, around 3000 B.C. In Denmark, on the other hand, the Neolithic period covers the time 2500 to 1500 B.C., and among the Australian aborigines, neolithic culture never emerged at all.

The Neolithic period is important because it marks the most important change in human culture since the discovery of fire: the transition from food-gathering and hunter societies to food-producing societies. Food-gathering societies are dependent on wild life for their own existence; they either gather plants, insects, and small animals or hunt for game. In the Neolithic period the skills of domesticating animals, cultivating farmland, weaving cloth, and making pottery were developed. This led to the emergence of two new kinds of societies: pastoral and agricultural ones.

Religions of pastoral societies tend to be "Uranian," i.e., the prime religious symbol is the sky, which is the abode of the gods. We have already considered in some detail examples of pastoral societies in the Nuer and Dinka. These societies tend to view the power of their deities in the sky, sun, thunder, and storm, which are the forces with which herders are much concerned. Such societies and their gods are usually patriarchal. This religious pattern has been transmitted to many early civilizations. The Greek Zeus and Roman Jupiter, the Semitic Jehovah, Indra and Varuna of the Aryans, Thor of the Scandinavians are examples of "High Gods" of the sky related to pastoral religion.

On the other hand, agricultural or planter religions tend to stress the recurring cycles of springtime and harvest, of the regenerative and reproductive powers of nature. The prime symbol is the earth rather than the sky, the feminine rather than the masculine. The basic concern is with birth, fertility, growth, and maturation. Here, a goddess often assumes preeminence over a god. In various ways agricultural religions have oriented themselves toward symbols of a great goddess—"Mother of the Wheat" or "Mother of the Maize." In later religions the "Great Mother" appears as the Greek Diana, Demeter, Hecate, and Persephone, the Roman Cybele, the Indian Kali. She is Inanna to the Sumerians, Ishtar to the Assyrians and Babylonians, Isis to the Egyptians.

A modern poet, Robert Graves, has written the following poem in her honor:

THE WHITE GODDESS

All saints revile her, and all sober men
Ruled by the God Apollo's golden mean—
In scorn of which we sailed to find her
In distant regions likeliest to hold her
Whom we desired above all things to know,
Sister of the mirage and echo.

It was a virtue not to stay,
To go our headstrong and heroic way
Seeking her out at the volcano's head
Among pack ice, or where the track had faded
Beyond the cavern of the seven sleepers:
Whose broad high brow was white as any leper's,
Whose eyes were blue, with rowan-berry lips,
With hair curled honey-coloured to white hips.

Egyptian bird deity, c. 4000 B.C., depicting the female form with uplifted arms and the head of a bird. (Courtesy of the Brooklyn Museum.)

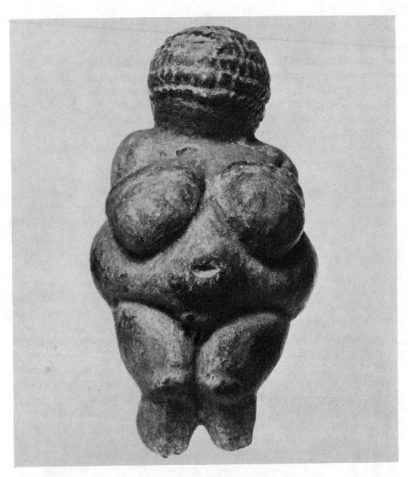

The paleolithic "Venus" of Willendorf, Austria, an obvious fertility figure.
(Courtesy of the American Museum of Natural History.)

> Green sap of Spring in the young wood a-stir
> Will celebrate the Mountain Mother,
> And every song-bird shout awhile for her;
> But we are gifted, even in November
> Rawest of seasons, with so huge a sense
> Of her nakedly worn magnificence
> We forget cruelty and past betrayal,
> Heedless of where the next bright bolt may fall.[3]

A key image of agricultural religion is the seed which dies in the earth, only to come to life again as a burgeoning crop: The pattern of death and rebirth in endless alternation, just as the life of summer always follows the death of winter, is celebrated in myth and ritual.

Human and animal sacrifice played a significant role at times in agricultural religion. In order to influence, encourage, and partici-

3. Robert Graves, *Collected Poems*. Reprinted by permission of Collins-Knowlton-Wing, Inc. Copyright © 1961 by Robert Graves.

pate in life processes that are fecund and bounteous, agricultural communities sometimes made ritual offerings of human beings, whose death was believed to release the powers of life and fertility in the community. The patterns of planter religion later merged with those of archaic civilizations.

In ancient times tribes of war-like peoples wandered throughout Europe and Asia, frequently conquering local inhabitants and establishing their own culture and religion. Their influence plays an important part in the religious history of India as well as in northern Europe. The Celts, the Teutons, and the Slavs are tribes whose religious practices made a strong impression on the development of later religions in Europe. The mythology of the Teutons has, along with that of the Greeks, become part of the literary lore of Western man.

ANCIENT RELIGIONS OF NORTHERN EUROPE

The Celts migrated to Germany, France, Spain, Italy, Greece and England. Their priests were called Druids who cultivated religious practices establishing close relations between man and natural objects, particularly trees. At one period they evidently practiced human sacrifice.

The Teutons have provided Western man with an exciting mythology contained in two works, the *Poetic Edda* and the *Prose Edda*. Here we learn of one of the oldest of the gods, Ziu, who is related to the Greek Zeus, the Roman Jupiter, and the Dyaus Pitar of the Vedic gods. Thor is the god of thunder, Wodan or Odin is the god of war who welcomes warriors who have fallen in battle to Valhalla where heroes lived after death in a great hall in the sky. Freyr is the god of summer and fertility, Freyja is his sister and wife.

Teutonic myths contain an account of the creation of the world and of the end of the world. The world began when an original state of cold, heat, lime and slush generated a cosmic giant named Ymir. Another giant, Buri, who had been frozen in the ice, was freed by the cosmic cow Andumla. Buri's offspring slew Ymir and made the parts of the world from the parts of his body; earth from his flesh, the sea from his blood and so forth. The first man and woman Askr and Embla were made from two trees.

The world order now consisted of Utgard where the frost giants lived, Askgard where the gods lived, Nldgard where man lived, and Hel, the abode of the dead, except for heroes who went to Valhalla. However, the time would come when this order was expected to disintegrate; a final holocaust would take place in which the gods would be defeated by forces of chaos—giants and other creatures from Hel and regions at the end of the world. Man would be extinguished in a general conflagration that marked the Götterdammerung, or the death of the gods.

Afterwards, a new earth would emerge out of the chaos and two survivors of the holocaust would be the origin of a new race of man that would establish a more benign social order.

The Slavs possessed a religious orientation toward nature and the virtues of a warrior society similar to that of the Celts and Teu-

Sakkara Pyramid, Egypt. (Photo by Fritz Henle, from Monkmeyer Press Photo Service.)

tons. Christianity later became the dominant religion of these Indo-European tribes, but traces of the earlier religious practices and beliefs remain to this day as part of the heritage of Western man.

THE RELIGIONS OF THE ARCHAIC CIVILIZATIONS

As used in this book, the word "civilization" is not a synonym for culture. A culture is the totality of learned, socially transmitted behavior present in a human society. By definition, every society without exception has "a culture." "Civilization," however, refers to a certain kind of social and cultural organization that emerged in the Near East around 3000 B.C. Two basic characteristics of civilizations are the use of writing and the greater differentiation of the parts of the social complex when compared to a primitive society. The development of cities, urbanization, is also a mark of civilization. Finally, the development of metallurgy in the Bronze Age beginning around 3000 B.C. and the Iron Age beginning around 2000 B.C. coincides with the rise of civilization.

During this period from 3000 to 536 B.C. there emerged in the Tigris-Euphrates valley a succession of great archaic civilizations —the Sumerian, the Babylonian, the Assyrian, and the Chaldean. In the region of the Nile during the same period, the Egyptian civilization dominated from 3000 B.C. until it succumbed to the Persians in 525 B.C. These civilizations exhibit a common religious form in which the political structure and the divine structure of the cosmos are considered as congruent parts of an external sacred pattern and process. The human political world is viewed as a microcosm of the divine macrocosm.

The religions of these Near Eastern civilizations represent a fusion of religious forms operative in agricultural societies with forms concerned with the political life of the community centered in the great cities. The city and the surrounding areas devoted to farming were parts of an integrated social system. In Mesopotamia many of the townspeople worked their own fields and "the life of all was regulated by a calendar which harmonized society's progress through the year with the succession of the seasons." [4]

The Sumerians worshiped a pantheon of gods that included An, a sky god; Enlil, a god of the atmosphere who conferred on the king his authority; Enki, sovereign of the fields. Dumuzi is a hero who later assumes the role of a fertility god, representing the dying and reviving vegetation. According to myth, he is the consort of Inanna, the love goddess, who sends him to the region of the dead to abide there in her place. With the Assyrians and Babylonians, Inanna is called Ishtar or Astarte, and Dumuzi is Tammuz, for whom the Bible notes that "there sat women weeping" (Ezek. 8:14).

A famous document has been preserved from Babylonian times called the *Enuma Elish,* the epic of creation. It tells how the gods emerge from the primeval waters of Apsu and Tiamat. Tiamat later assumes the role of a monster whom the gods ask Marduk to destroy. He finally does so, and from Tiamat's body he makes the world and also creates man. As the controller of the destiny of the world, he founds Babylon and its temple and becomes its national god.

The creation myth is connected with certain ritual ceremonies in which agricultural and political myths are combined. Thus, the Babylonian king begins his reign on New Year's day in the month of Nisan at the time of the spring rains. Each year at this time, the Akitu festival was usually performed. It apparently included ceremonies where the king was divested of his crown, ring, and scepter, only to be reinvested with them after he declared his innocence of wrongdoing before Marduk. This ceremony is correlated with other symbolic acts acknowledging the threat of chaos. The *Enuma Elish* was read and ritual enactment of Marduk's victory over Tiamat was performed. Evidently at the end of this sacred festival, the king and queen engaged in ritual intercourse symbolizing the union of Ishtar and Tammuz, which ensured the continued fertility of the earth.

The religions of the archaic civilizations of the Near East were centered in the idea of kingship. The king was the mediating point that joined the world of the gods and the world of human society into a single dynamic interacting process. Through the agency of the king, human society functioned according to the norms and patterns decreed by the gods and which the gods also exemplified in their relations to one another. Thus the political patterns in human society reflected the pattern of authority that also operated among the gods themselves.

Henri Frankfort, a renowned scholar in this area, points to an important difference between the idea of kingship in the Mesopotamian civilizations and in Egypt.[5] In Mesopotamia, the king was the

4. Henri Frankfort, *The Birth of Civilization in the Near East,* London, Williams and Norgate, 1951, p. 58.

5. Henri Frankfort, *Kingship and the Gods,* Chicago, The University of Chicago Press, 1948.

agent of the gods and ruled in their name. But he himself was regarded as human and subject to death. For example, in a famous
Babylonian document we learn the story of Gilgamesh, a great king,
part divine and part mortal, who performs various heroic feats and,
when his friend dies, sets out on a search for eternal life. He finally
finds the plant of eternal life, but before he can partake of it, a
snake snatches it away. In this myth both the greatness and essential finitude of man are expressed. Through the king the will of the
gods is imposed on the government of the city-state. Nevertheless,
an essential difference between divinity and mankind, including the
king, is also declared. Only the gods are immortal. The human king,
representing his people, must die.

In Egypt, on the other hand, the pharaoh himself was regarded as
one of the gods who had descended among men. In the civilizations
of the Near East some distance between the divine and human
worlds is maintained. In the Egyptian scheme, the social order,
through the authority of the divine pharaoh, has itself been divin-
ized. The Egyptian pantheon of gods included Horus, depicted in
human shape with a falcon's head. He was the god of political authority, and the pharaoh was sometimes regarded as the kingly
incarnation of Horus on earth. The development of the cult of Isis
and Osiris is of special interest. According to the myth, Osiris is
killed by his brother Seth. Isis, his wife, mourns over him and
through magic spells gets herself impregnated by her dead husband. She gives birth to Horus, to whom the gods give the rights
and dignity originally belonging to his father. Osiris is then restored
to life and made sovereign over the realm of the dead. It seems
likely that the cult was directed toward the kingship motif, in which
the dying pharaoh assumes the role of Osiris and his successor that
of Horus.

One fascinating interlude in Egyptian religion concerns the attempt of the Egyptian Pharaoh Amenhotep IV (Akhenaten) to insti-
tute a monotheistic cult centered around the worship of the sun disc
under the name of Aton. The cult was short-lived and was destroyed
by the Egyptian priests on the death of Akhenaten.

A similar cultural stage was also reached in Central and South
America at a later period. By 2000 B.C. the inhabitants had made
the transition from hunting to agricultural patterns and thereby entered the Neolithic stage of culture. From this culture emerged
three great civilizations: the Aztec of Mexico, the Mayan of Guate-
mala and the Yucatan peninsula, and the Inca of Peru. Let us briefly
consider one of them—the Aztec.

The Aztecs reigned from about 1325 until their defeat by the
Spaniards in 1521. Their pantheon included Ometecuhtli, the supreme god; Tezcatlipoca, originally a tribal god who also assumed
the form of the war god Huitzilopochtli; Xiuhtecuhtli, the lord of
fire; and Tlazolteotl, a "great goddess" figure similar to Ishtar
and Inanna. The most interesting god to moderns is Quetzalcoatl,
the "plumed serpent." According to myth, Quetzalcoatl was a culture hero who brought the arts of civilization to the Mexican tribes.
Later, during the time of the Aztecs, he became the god of the wind

and of heaven at night. Finally, he left his people as an old man and wandered to the east, where he cremated himself and became the morning star. However, he had promised to return in the form of a man. The Aztecs made the crucial mistake of believing that the prophecy had been fulfilled in the coming of the Spanish conquistador Cortez; for this error they paid dearly.

The Aztecs are especially remembered for the intensity with which they performed human sacrifices. Here the motifs and memories, which in the other archaic civilizations pointed to ancient practices largely sublimated into symbolic images, erupted with literal ferocity. It is alleged, for example, that twelve thousand prisoners were killed at one time during the reign of Montezuma II. It was believed that through these sacrifices the intimate relationship among human life in the city, the forces of nature, and the realm of the gods was maintained.

The religious forms exhibited by the archaic civilizations of Mesopotamia, Egypt, and the Americas are an impressive achievement. They provide an important historical bridge between the religions of tribal societies—hunters, pastoralists, and agriculturalists—and the religions of the succeeding civilizations which still exist today as living cultural forces.

GREEK RELIGION

As we turn from the religions of the archaic civilizations, Greek religion deserves special notice. The Greeks produced a remarkable culture that has influenced Western civilization far in excess of the actual material power it exerted during its period of ascendancy. Indeed, in an important sense, it is responsible for the ideal of civilization as a social form cultivating a reasonable and humane life. As Toynbee notes: "Interpreted literally, the word 'civilization' ought to mean an attempt to attain the kind of culture that had been attained by citizens of a Graeco-Roman . . . city state." [6]

Greek religion is the product of a fusion of the cults of a native population, the Pelasgians, with those of northern invaders. Behind the pantheon of gods with which most Western students are familiar are rituals and practices tied in with tribal patterns of thought and behavior. Homer, the author of the two great epic poems, *The Iliad* and *The Odyssey,* seems to be responsible for the formalization of various ritual beliefs into a systematic pantheon of gods in which each divinity possesses a distinctive individuality.

The pantheon of gods that emerged into view during the classical period included Zeus, the god of the sky, and Hera his wife; Ares, god of war; Hephaestus, the god of fire and of the smithy; Pallas Athena, goddess of wisdom who was the guiding power of Athens; Apollo, the sun god who presided over music and is the exemplar of calm, clear reason, and light.

The Olympian gods comprise the Uranian element in Greek religion which, during its classical period, is the dominant one. However, the other elements are also important. First are cults directed

6. Arnold Toynbee, *Reconsiderations,* New York, Oxford, 1961, p. 273.

The Temple of Apollo at Delphi, Greece, the seat of the famous Delphic oracle.

toward the Chthonoi, spirits who live in the dark recesses of the earth. They are connected with fertility and death, since the earth is the matrix of living things but also the place in which the bodies of men are buried. The chthonian spirits thus have the qualities of demons, hobgoblins, gods of the night, darkness, terror, and death. These beings are not necessarily evil in any absolute sense, but they represent the darker passions and fears of man contrasted with his aspiration after light, clarity, and freedom. We thus can speak of Uranian and chthonian elements in religion. The Greeks acknowledged both, as when Pindar writes: "O ye gods above and reverend Chthonoi who dwell in tombs."

The other non-Olympian element in Greek religion is the presence of various "mystery religions." We do not know if any or all of these cults are indigenous to Greece, or foreign intrusions, perhaps from Asia Minor. Three of them are of special importance: Orphism, the Dionysian cult, and the Eleusinian mysteries.

The Eleusinian mysteries celebrate the well-known story of Demeter and her daughter Kore, who was abducted by Hades, god of the dead, and taken to his nether realm. Demeter, one form of the Great Mother of fertility, mourned and did not allow the agricultural realm to rejuvenate itself. Zeus prevailed on Hades to give Kore up, but because she had eaten a pomegranate seed while below, she was forced to return to Hades each year. Winter and summer were the seasons of her descent and return. The rites of this mystery cult enabled the members to feel that they were participating in the divine events proclaimed in the myth. Thus, *on the evening of their arrival at Eleusis, the initiates broke off their dances and rejoicings when they were told that Kore had been carried away. Torch in hand, crying and lamenting, they wandered everywhere, searching for Kore. Suddenly a herald announced that Helios had revealed where Kore was; and again all was gaiety, music, dancing. The myth of Demeter and Kore became contemporary once more; the rape of Kore, Demeter's laments, take place here and now, and it is by virtue of this nearness of the Goddesses, and finally of their presence, that the initiate (mystes) will have the unforgettable experience of initiation.*[7]

The cult of Dionysus cultivated frenzied and orgiastic emotions and dances and is often contrasted with the calm and clarity of Apollo. According to one myth associated with this cult, Dionysus was a son of Zeus, born from his father's body when his mother died before giving him birth. Another myth tells how Zagreus (an early form of Dionysus) was torn apart and devoured by divine beings called Titans. The Orphic cult has a similar story to tell about Orpheus.

These mystery cults apparently promised the initiate access to a kind of immortality not available to the outsider. Other cults that influenced Mediterranean cultures include the mysteries of the Phrygian Cybele and Attis and the Egyptian Isis and Osiris; and later, in the second century A.D., the cult of the Persian light-god Mithras. One important feature of these cults is that they reveal a growing independence from their original cultural matrix. Most of the mystery cults are not tied to a specific tribe, or nation, but form universal societies composed of members from a variety of places.

RELIGIONS OF ROMAN CIVILIZATION

The religious traditions of Rome are of importance because Roman civilization formed the soil out of which the Western societies of the modern world have emerged. The religious practices of the ancient Romans were centered around the family and civic life. Through symbol and rite a respect was paid to the numinous powers and forces believed to be present in natural phenomena and in hearth and home. Rudolf Otto coined the term "numinous" to characterize the feeling of religious awe on the basis of this Roman usage (see p. 22).

Later the numina, which at first were felt as vague forces in archaic symbols and rituals, took on more specific forms in the familiar pantheon of Roman gods which were in many instances patterned after Greek models. Thus Jupiter is the sky god: Juno, his consort; Diana, the moon goddess; Neptune, the sea god; Mars, the war god.

The Roman approach to religion was profoundly affected by the emergence of the empire in the first century B.C. As the Romans

7. Mircea Eliade, *Rites and Symbols of Initiation*, New York, Harper Torchbooks, 1965, p. 110.

conquered surrounding territories, contact with alien cultural patterns led to a cosmopolitan approach to religion. Indeed, it is interesting to observe that the root word for religion is of Roman derivation (see pp. 19–20). Use of the noun form to refer to a phenomenon called "religio" became prominent during this period when Rome was making contact through conquest with many different cultures. This led to some interest in comparative problems, as philosophers noted similarities between the gods of different religions and cultures.

Among the educated Romans two attitudes are particularly noteworthy. One is skepticism about the truth of any religious system. References to the gods are thus treated by many Romans of the period as poetical expressions and not as matters of conviction. Also present among some philosophers is a syncretist attempt to compose a comprehensive religious system in which gods from a number of different cultures are included. The Emperor Julian attempted without success to impose such a system as the official religion of the empire as a whole.

One Roman philosopher, Varo, summarized the various forms of Roman religion under three headings: mythological religion, represented by the gods referred to in the writings of poets and sometimes worshiped by numerous groups of the populace; civic religion, represented by those rites that maintained loyalty to the Roman state; natural religion, represented by the speculations of philosophers like the Platonists and the Stoics.

The emergence of the empire created for the Romans the problem of developing a sense of loyalty to Roman authority as the controlling center of its far-flung political structure. Rites of obeisance to the emperor as a divine personage were instituted as a supplement to other existing religious practices. These rites seem to have been the result of a pragmatic desire to achieve a form of political unity rather than of the deeply felt convictions among large numbers of people.

In the fourth century A.D. the Roman Empire attempted to solve its problems of finding a uniting center by adopting Christianity, first as simply one among many acceptable religions, and then as the official religion of the empire. The Roman genius for order on both the political and intellectual level provided patterns of systematic thought which are part of the heritage bequeathed to the modern Western world. In many ways the modern concern with the problem of "religion" has its roots in the Roman experience.

HISTORIC RELIGIONS OF LATER CIVILIZATIONS

We are now ready to consider the religions that are our primary concern in this book. The word "historic" is used for want of a better word to designate religions that have appeared fairly recently so far as the total span of man's existence on this planet is concerned, and which continue to exert a significant influence on contemporary affairs. These religions are grouped according to the three geographical areas in which each of them originated or is presently active: Jainism, Hinduism, and Buddhism as religions in India;

Confucianism, Hinduism, Mahayana Buddhism, and Shinto in the Far East; Judaism, Christianity, and Islam in the Near East, Europe, and the Americas.

These are the so-called "living" religions that continue to be vital factors in contemporary societies. These religions have been selected for study in this book partially on the basis of their influence in terms of numbers of adherents. Numerous contemporary cults with small memberships are also worthy of detailed study, but we suggest this be deferred until the patterns of the larger religious complexes are mastered. This book attempts to assist the reader in this introductory purpose.

These religions have been selected for study because they are significant constituents of societies that command attention in the international scene. Religion is more than its social form; yet, as we have seen, it is deeply involved in a social matrix and we must admit that the criterion by which we identify a given religion is often its social manifestation.

However, the historic religions reveal a high degree of autonomy and cultural differentiation; this means that the structures of the historic religions can be examined apart from their social matrix as well as in connection with it. The point may seem obvious, but we hope that the preceding account has shown that this feature of the historic religions is a new and distinctive one. By contrast, the tribal religions of primitive societies are integral parts of the social nexus that is the tribe. The religion is almost literally nonexistent when considered apart from its tribe. For example, one could hardly today become a follower of Dinka religion without becoming a full member of a Dinka tribe. The same situation is true of the religions of the archaic civilizations, which were profoundly connected with the political order and perished with the dissolution of that order.

In many ways the historic religions perpetuate features we have observed in the archaic religions. However, they also focus more sharply on individual goals (like salvation of the soul, release from the wheel of time, etc.) that can be differentiated from social concerns.

Behind this growth in autonomy and independence from the political order is a breakthrough in thought and insight which took place in the first millennium before Christ. The philosopher Karl Jaspers calls attention to the fact that the cultural foundation of basic norms, models, insights, and visions which still influence contemporary man appeared during a period of time that he calls the axial period. He writes: "In the years centering around 500 B.C.—from 800 to 200—the spiritual foundations of humanity were laid, simultaneously and independently, in China, India, Persia, Palestine, and Greece. And these are the foundations upon which humanity still subsists today." [8] In the following chart we have enlarged Jaspers' time boundaries to include the following religious and philosophical figures.

8. Karl Jaspers, *The Origin and Goal of History*, London, Routledge, 1953, p. 1.

THE AXIAL PERIOD

Unknown authors of the Vedas	before 1000 B.C.
Moses	1250 B.C.
Unknown authors of the Upanishads	800–600 B.C.
The Hebrew Prophets	800–400 B.C.
Confucius	551–479 B.C.
Zoroaster	c. 660 B.C.
Lao-Tze	c. 604–517 B.C.
Mahavira	599–527 B.C.
Gautama Buddha	560–480 B.C.
Socrates	470–399 B.C.
Plato	428–348 B.C.
Jesus	4 B.C.–29 A.D.
Mani	216–277 A.D.
Mohammed	570–632 A.D.

While building on past religious forms from primitive and archaic societies, these emerging religions and philosophies have developed a new understanding of themselves and their relation to society in which we as moderns are still participating.

Some observations by Arnold Toynbee are important at this point. He acknowledges that when he began his monumental study of civilizations, he thought of religion as one of the cultural forms through which a given civilization could be studied. However, as certain religions—Christianity, Mahayana Buddhism, for example—were found to persist as autonomous entities after their germinating civilization had died or been abandoned, he revised his judgment. He now argues that the historic religions "catch a new vision of the spiritual presences, higher than man, in which these presences are no longer seen through the medium of human economic and political needs and activities but are seen as direct powers that are not implicated *ex officio* in their local worshippers' human concerns." Thus he concludes:

The higher religions have made their epiphany in the course of the age of the civilizations; and if we take them at their adherents' valuation of them we shall find in them alternative fields of study that will be more illuminating than civilizations because, in the higher religions, we shall be studying man's most important activity.[9]

Since the term "higher" religions conveys an unfortunate suggestion of superiority, we prefer here to call them "historic" religions which have been important in the development of the civilizations of China, India, Europe, and the Americas. We are now ready to embark on an exploration of the growth and development of these religions in the course of historical time. It is a story full of important insights for a proper understanding of how man has in the recent historical past interpreted his world. Let us begin.

9. Toynbee, op. cit., pp. 83, 218.

For a survey of theories about religion see:

de Vries, Jan, *The Study of Religion,* Kees W. Bolle, trans., New York, Harcourt Brace Jovanovich, paperback ed., 1967.

Evans-Pritchard, E. E., *Theories of Primitive Religion,* New York, Oxford University Press, 1965.

For a history of anthropological schools see:

Lowie, Robert, *The History of Ethnological Theory,* London, Harrap, 1937.

For a popular survey of anthropological studies see:

Hays, H. R., *From Ape to Angel,* New York, Capricorn Books, paperback ed., 1964.

For representative examples of 19th-century studies of religion that are still useful see:

Frazer, James, *The Golden Bough,* 13 vols., New York, St. Martin's, 1890–1936. Cf. Edmund Leach, "Frazer and Malinowski," *Encounter, 25,* no. 5 (November, 1965), 24–36.

Marett, R. R., *The Threshold of Religion,* London, Methuen, 1909.

Tylor, Edward B., *Religion in Primitive Culture,* New York, Harper & Row, paperback ed., 1958 (originally published in 1871).

For the presence of "high gods" in primitive cultures see:

Eliade, Mircea, "Australian Religions: An Introduction: Part I," *History of Religions,* Vol. 6, Chicago, The University of Chicago Press, pp. 108–134.

Lang, Andrew, "God (Primitive and Savage)," in J. Hastings, ed., *Encyclopedia of Religion and Ethics,* New York, Scribner, 1908–1927.

Pettazzoni, R., "The Supreme Being: Phenomenological Structure and Historical Development," in M. Eliade and J. Kitagawa, eds., *The History of Religions: Essays in Methodology,* Chicago, The University of Chicago Press, 1959.

For the contemporary emphasis on description see:

Beattie, John, *Other Cultures,* New York, Free Press, paperback ed., 1964.

Eliade, Mircea, "The History of Religions in Retrospect: 1912 and After," *The Quest,* Chicago, The University of Chicago Press, 1969, pp. 12–36.

———, "The Quest for the 'Origins of Religion'," *History of Religions,* Vol. 4, Chicago, The University of Chicago Press, pp. 154–169.

Evans-Pritchard, E. E., *Social Anthropology,* London, Cohen & West, 1951.

For discussions of the study of religion see:

Eliade, Mircea, and Joseph Kitagawa, eds., *The History of Religions: Essays in Methodology,* Chicago, The University of Chicago Press, 1959.

Kitagawa, Joseph, ed., *The History of Religions: Essays in the Problem of Understanding,* Chicago, The University of Chicago Press, 1967.

For the psychological approach to religion see:

Allport, Gordon, *The Individual and His Religion,* New York, Macmillan, paperback ed., 1960.

BIBLIOGRAPHY
Approaches to the Study of Religion

Erikson, Erik, *Identity: Youth & Crises,* London, Faber, 1968.

Freud, Sigmund, *Civilization and Its Discontents; Future of an Illusion; Totem and Taboo;* many editions. See, for example, *Standard Edition of the Complete Psychological Works of Sigmund Freud,* London, Hogarth, 1961.

Jung, Carl, *Modern Man in Search of a Soul,* London, Routledge, 1958.

Jung, Carl, and C. Kerenyi, *Introduction to a Science of Mythology,* London, Routledge, 1951.

Neumann, Eric, *The Origins and the History of Consciousness,* 2 vols., New York, Harper & Row, paperback ed., 1962.

For the sociological approach see:

Firth, Raymond, *Essays on Social Organization and Values,* London, Athlone Press, 1964.

O'Dea, Thomas, *The Sociology of Religion,* Englewood Cliffs, N.J., Prentice-Hall, paperback ed., 1966.

Parsons, Talcott, *Theories of Society,* New York, Free Press, 1965.

Robertson, Roland, *The Sociological Interpretation of Religion,* Oxford, Blackwell, 1970.

Weber, Max, "The Social Psychology of the World Religions," in H. H. Gerth and C. Wright Mills, eds., *From Max Weber,* New York, Oxford University Press, 1946.

————, *The Sociology of Religion,* Boston, Beacon Press, paperback ed., 1963.

For the historical approach to religion see:

Volumes of *History of Religions,* Chicago, The University of Chicago Press.

For the comparative approach to religion see:

Eliade, Mircea, *Patterns in Comparative Religion,* New York, Sheed, 1958.

————, *Shamanism,* New York, Bollingen, 1964.

Kristensen, W. Brede, *The Meaning of Religion,* Hague, Martinus Nijhoff, 1960.

Littleton, C. Scott, *The New Comparative Mythology: An Anthropological Assessment of the Theories of Georges Dumezal,* Berkeley, Calif., University of California Press, 1966.

Van Der Leeuw, Gerardus, *Religion in Essence and Manifestation,* London, G. Allen, 1938.

Wach, Joachim, *Types of Religious Experience,* Chicago, University of Chicago Press, 1957.

For the hermeneutical approach to religion see the bibliography for "Religion as Action and Meaning," below.

For the problem of cultural perspectives see:

Macintyre, Alasdair, "Is Understanding Religion Compatible with Believing?" in John Hick, ed., *Faith and the Philosophers,* New York, St. Martin's, 1966, pp. 115–155.

Toward a
Definition of Religion

For the problems of definition in general see:

Robinson, Richard, *Definition,* New York, Oxford University Press, 1954.

For definitions of religion with good bibliographies see:

Geertz, Clifford, "Religion as a Cultural System," in Michael Banton, ed., *Anthropological Approaches to the Study of Religion,* London, Tavistock Publications, 1966, pp. 1–46.

Spiro, Melford E., "Religion: Problems of Definition and Explanation," in Michael Banton, ed., *Anthropological Approaches to the Study of Religion,* London, Tavistock Publications, 1966, pp. 85–126.

Baird, Robert, "Interpretive Categories and the History of Religions," *History and Theory, 8* (1968), 17–30.

For the definition of religion as a reference to the superempirical see:

Glock, Charles Y., and Rodney N. Stark, *Religion and Society in Tension,* Chicago, University of Chicago Press, 1965.

For the definition of religion as a reference to the sacred see:

Caillois, Roger, *Man and the Sacred,* New York, Free Press, 1959.

Durkheim, Emile, *The Elementary Forms of the Religious Life,* New York, Free Press, paperback ed., 1965.

Eliade, Mircea, *The Sacred and the Profane,* New York, Harper & Row, paperback ed., 1961.

Nisbet, Robert, "The Sacred," *The Sociological Tradition,* London, Heinemann, 1966, pp. 221–263.

For the definition of religion as a reference to ultimacy see:

Luckmann, Thomas, *The Invisible Religion,* New York, Macmillan, 1967.

Parsons, Talcott, "Religion in a Modern Pluralistic Society," *Review of Religious Research, 7* (Spring, 1966), 125–146.

Tillich, Paul, *Christianity and the Encounter of the World Religions,* Chicago, University of Chicago Press, 1960.

For the study of ritual see:

Bettelheim, Bruno, *Symbolic Wounds,* New York, Collier, paperback ed., 1962.

Emmet, Dorothy, "Religion and the Social Anthropology of Religion: II," *Theoria to Theory, 3* (January, 1969), 33–44.

Firth, R., *Tikopia: Ritual and Belief,* London, G. Allen, 1967.

———, *The Work of the Gods in Tikopia,* London, Athlone Press, 1967.

Goody, J., "Religion and Ritual: The Definition Problem," *British Journal of Sociology, 12,* 143–164.

Middleton, John, ed., *Gods and Rituals,* New York, Natural History Press, 1967.

Turner, Victor, *The Ritual Process,* London, Routledge, 1969.

For a survey of the ritual myth school see:

Fontenrose, J. E., *The Ritual Theory of Myth,* Berkeley, Calif., University of California Press, 1966.

For discussions of functional theory see:

Emmet, Dorothy, *Function, Purpose and Powers,* New York, Macmillan, 1958.

Merton, Robert K., *On Theoretical Sociology,* New York, Free Press, paperback ed., 1967.

Religion as
Action and Meaning

Radcliffe-Brown, A. R., *Structure and Function in Primitive Society,* New York, Free Press, paperback ed., 1952.

For discussions of expressive symbolism and "play" theory see:

Beattie, John, *Other Cultures,* New York, Free Press, paperback ed., 1964, chap. 12.

Huizinga, John, *Homo Ludens,* Boston, Beacon Press, paperback ed., 1950.

Langer, Susanne, *Philosophy in a New Key,* New York, New American Library, paperback ed., 1964.

Pieper, Josef, *Leisure, the Basis of Culture,* London, Faber, 1952.

For discussions of "mana" see:

Firth, R., "The Analysis of Mana: An Empirical Approach," *Tikopia: Ritual and Belief,* London, G. Allen, 1967, pp. 174–194.

For discussions of primitive views of "soul" see:

Firth, R., "The Fate of the Soul," *Tikopia: Ritual and Belief,* London, G. Allen, 1967, pp. 330–353.

For discussions of Totemism see:

Lévi-Strauss, Claude, *Totemism,* Boston, Beacon Press, 1963.

Worsley, Peter, "Groote Eylandt Totémism and Le Totemisme aujourd'hui," in E. Leach, ed., *The Structural Study of Myth and Totemism,* London, Tavistock Publications, 1967, pp. 141–160.

For discussions of magic see:

Beattie, John, *Other Cultures,* New York, Free Press, 1964.

Douglas, Mary, *Purity and Danger,* London, Routledge, 1966.

Evans-Pritchard, E. E., *Witchcraft, Oracles and Magic among the Azande,* New York, Oxford University Press, 1940.

Goode, William, *Religion Among the Primitives,* New York, Free Press, paperback ed., 1951.

Malinowski, B., *Magic, Science and Religion,* New York, Doubleday, paperback ed., 1954.

Nadel, S., "Malinowski on Magic and Religion," in R. Firth, ed., *Man and Culture,* London, Routledge, 1957, pp. 189–208.

Religion as Symbolic Expression

For the study of symbolism see:

Cassirer, Ernst, *The Philosophy of Symbolic Forms,* 3 vols., New Haven, Conn., Yale, 1954–1957.

Geertz, Clifford, "Religion as a Cultural System," in Michael Banton, ed., *Anthropological Approaches to the Study of Religion,* London, Tavistock Publications, 1966, pp. 1–46.

Langer, Susanne, *Philosophy in a New Key,* New York, New American Library, paperback ed., 1954.

For discussions of myth see:

Eliade, Mircea, *Myth and Reality,* New York, Harper & Row, paperback ed., 1963.

————, *Myths, Dreams and Mysteries,* New York, Collins, paperback ed., 1968.

Emmet, Dorothy, "Religion and the Social Anthropology of Religion: III," *Theoria to Theory, 3* (April, 1969), 42–55.

Long, Charles, "Religion and Mythology: A Critical Review of Some Recent Discussions," in *History of Religions,* Vol. 1, Chicago, University of Chicago Press, pp. 322–331.

Malinowski, B., *Myth in Primitive Society,* New York, Norton, 1926.

Middleton, John, ed., *Myth and Cosmos,* New York, Natural History Press, 1967.

Studies by Lévi-Strauss on structuralism:

Lévi-Strauss, Claude, *The Savage Mind,* London, Weidenfeld & Nicholson, 1967.

————, *The Scope of Anthropology,* London, Cape, 1967.

————, "The Story of Asdiwal," in E. Leach, ed., *The Structural Study of Myth and Totemism,* London, Tavistock Publications, 1967, pp. 1–47.

————, *Structural Anthropology,* New York, Basic Books, 1963.

Introductions to the study of structuralism:

Barthes, Roland, *Elements of Semiology,* London, Cape, 1967.

Charbonnier, C., *Conversations with Claude Lévi-Strauss,* London, Cape, 1969.

Lane, Michael, ed., *Structuralism: A Reader,* London, Cape, 1970.

Leach, Edmund, *Lévi-Strauss,* New York, Collins, 1970.

For a discussion of Nuer society see:

Evans-Pritchard, E. E., *Nuer,* New York, Oxford University Press, 1940.

————, *Nuer Religion,* New York, Oxford University Press, 1956.

For a discussion of Dinka society see:

Lienhardt, Godfrey, *Divinity and Experience,* New York, Oxford University Press, 1961.

For the study of preliterate religion in general see:

Birket-Smith, Kaj, *Primitive Man and His Ways,* New York, New American Library, paperback ed., 1963.

Goode, William, *Religion Among the Primitives,* New York, Free Press, paperback ed., 1951.

Lessa, William, and Evan Vogt, eds., *A Reader in Comparative Religion,* New York, Harper & Row, 1965.

Lowie, Robert, *Primitive Religion,* New York, Liveright, 1924.

Radin, P., *Primitive Religion,* New York, Dover, paperback ed., 1957.

Wallace, Anthony, *Religion: An Anthropological View,* New York, Random House, 1966.

For a study of over-view and ethos see:

Geertz, Clifford, "Ethos, World-View and the Analysis of Sacred Symbols," *Antioch Review* (Winter, 1957–1958), 421–437.

For the concept of "primitive" see:

Montague, A., ed., *The Concept of Primitive,* New York, Free Press, paperback ed., 1968.

For discussions of the problem of the preliterate "mind," in addition to those by Lévi-Strauss, see:

Boas, Franz, *The Mind of Primitive Man,* New York, Free Press, paperback ed., 1965.

Durkheim, E., and Marcel Maas, *Primitive Classification,* Chicago, University of Chicago Press, 1967.

Levy-Bruhl, Lucien, *How Natives Think,* New York, Washington Square Press, Pocket Books, paperback ed., 1966.

————, *Primitive Mentality,* Boston, Beacon Press, paperback ed., 1966.

Primitive Religious
Systems

Radin, Paul, *Primitive Man as Philosopher,* New York, Dover, paperback ed., 1957.
————, *The World of Primitive Man,* New York, Grove Press, 1960.

The Historical Forms of Religion

For prehistoric religions and cultures see:

James, E. O., *Prehistoric Religion,* New York, Barnes & Noble, 1961.
Maringer, J., *The Gods of Prehistoric Man,* New York, Knopf, 1960.
Ucko, P. J., and A. Rosenfeld, *Paleolithic Cave Art,* New York, paperback ed., McGraw-Hill, 1967.

For religions of hunters, pastoralists, and agriculturalists see:

Eliade, Mircea, "Mother Earth and the Cosmic Hierogamies," *Myths, Dreams and Mysteries,* New York, Collins, 1968, pp. 156–192.
Sahlins, Marshall, *Tribesmen,* Englewood Cliffs, N.J., Prentice-Hall, paperback ed., 1968.
Service, Elman, *The Hunters,* Englewood Cliffs, N.J., Prentice-Hall, paperback ed., 1966.
Wolf, Eric, *Peasants,* Englewood Cliffs, N.J., Prentice-Hall, paperback ed., 1966.

For religions of archaic civilizations see:

Frankfort, Henri, John Wilson, and Thorkill Jacobson, *The Intellectual Adventure of Ancient Man,* Chicago, University of Chicago Press, 1946. Reprinted in paperback as *Before Philosophy,* Baltimore, Penguin, 1949.
Frankfort, Henri, *Kingship and the Gods,* Chicago, University of Chicago Press, 1948.
Kramer, S. N., *Sumerian Mythology,* New York, Harper & Row, paperback ed., 1960.
Wilson, John, *The Burden that Was Egypt,* Chicago, University of Chicago Press, 1951.

For religions of ancient Greece and Rome see:

Guthrie, W. K. C., *The Greeks and Their Gods,* Boston, Beacon Press, 1950.
Moore, C. H., *The Religious Thought of the Greeks,* Cambridge, Mass., Harvard, 1916.
Rose, H. J., *Religion in Greece and Rome,* New York, Harper & Row, paperback ed., 1961.

For the relationship between religions of primitive cultures and the religions of archaic and historic civilizations see:

Bellah, Robert, ed., *Religion and Progress in Modern Asia,* New York, Free Press, 1965.
Parsons, Talcott, *Societies,* Englewood Cliffs, N.J., Prentice-Hall, paperback ed., 1966.
Redfield, Robert, *The Primitive World and Its Transformations.* Ithaca, N.Y., Cornell, 1965.
Toynbee, Arnold, *Reconsiderations,* New York, Oxford University Press, 1961.

INDEX

72 73 74 75 7 6 5 4 3 2 1